Who's Coming For Dinner

More From Jeff's Kitchen

JEFF W. SUDDABY

PHOTOGRAPHY BY KELLY HOLINSHEAD

ISBN 978-0-9735008-2-0

Printed in Canada - First Edition

All Photographs Copyright© Kelly Holinshead
The Shutterbug Gallery www.kellytheshutterbug.ca

Creative Direction Johanne Stewart
www.dreamsbecomingreality.com

Who's Coming For Dinner

More From Jeff's Kitchen

JEFF W. SUDDABY

DEDICATION

This cookbook is affectionately dedicated to my Dad, Bill Suddaby.
They say "the apple doesn't fall far from the tree" and considering the
passion I have for food, I guess it's true.

Dad really loves food and every day since he retired, he cooks lunch for my
Mom, unless he drops by to hang out at the restaurant. He knows each
cook at 3 Guys by name and he enjoys visiting with the staff.
When one of the cooks whips up a meal for him, it really makes his day.

Thank you for the honesty and integrity that you've always shown and for
the great inspiration you've been to me in my life and in my work, Dad.
Love ya!

Jeff

ACKNOWLEDGMENTS

It took the effort and contribution of many people to launch this cookbook. I sincerely appreciate each and every person who offered a word of encouragement, an idea, or a helping hand to bring this second volume to life. So many people have worked tirelessly to help me make great strides toward my goals. From family to friends to loyal customers and business associates, it really was a collective effort. I offer a special thanks to:

Bev, my wife and friend, who lovingly listens, encourages, and supports me and keeps me on an even keel, and to my kids Jocelyn & Torin. I couldn't ask for a better family.

DeVonna Taylor, my administrator, for recognizing my drive and vision and supporting me as she works to help me pursue my dreams.

Tamara Marcus & Barry Marcus, of Generator Films, for all their work season after season on the television cooking show, *Who's Coming For Dinner*.

Sarah Vogelzang, Toronto Public Health Registered Dietitian, whose unflagging enthusiasm and focus on good health and good food is a natural fit for my 'Lifestyle Cooking' philosophy.

Sandi Munz, Trends Hair Studio, for the early morning appointments. Loved those lattes!

Kelly Holinshead, owner of The Shutterbug Gallery, whose tenacity in waiting for that one perfect shot speaks for itself in the outstanding photography in this book.

Johanne Stewart, Dreams Becoming Reality Marketing, whose superlative sense of style and design contributed so much to this project.

Dale Peacock, Peacock Ink Writing Services, for her way with words, and her upbeat attitude in her first year of working with us.

Randy Robinson, Your Independent Grocer, for providing great customer service and a wide variety of products. Every recipe in this cookbook can be made with ingredients from YIGs.

Al Servant, Drew Taylor, Jonathan MacKay and the entire staff at 3 Guys and a Stove. I am really fortunate to have this great team in my corner. They work diligently to keep things running smoothly, which allows me the freedom to follow my dreams.

The following people and companies have graciously allowed us to use their plates and accessories for food staging and photography purposes: Urban Rustic Living; Veranda Home & Garden Décor; Flotrons Tweed & Hickory; Huntsville Zellers; Saturday Afternoons in Huntsville; Mazooma; Patti Boothby; Jonathan MacKay; DeVonna Taylor; and Kelly Holinshead.

table of contents

INTRODUCTION

I'd like to offer a sincere thank you to everyone who bought my first cookbook. You made it a best seller! When you began asking when the next one was coming out, I started consulting with my team and thinking seriously about the direction we might take with the new edition. We wanted the cookbook to be consistent with what I serve in my restaurants and what I talk about on my television and radio shows, so we made sure that every recipe showcases my "lifestyle cooking " philosophy.

This new cookbook is designed to show you how to cook 'food with flavour' using ingredients that can be found in your local grocery store. I feel very strongly that you shouldn't have to trudge all over town, shopping for recipe ingredients, so I've designed my recipes to be made with things you can find at the local grocery store. Our market is not as diverse as that of larger metropolitan areas, but we can find everything we need in our local Loblaws store.

I really want to encourage parents to choose some recipes from this book and to spend some time in the kitchen with your kids. Remember that one day they'll be all grown up and inviting you over for dinner!

WHERE'S JEFF

When I'm not at one of the 3 Guys and a Stove locations, you might find me cooking at a wine and food show or teaching at one of the Loblaws cooking schools. Maybe I'm a guest chef, demonstrating a new and innovative dish on TV. Or, I could be taping segments for my radio show. When I travel with my family, we love eating out. New places inspire me and it always gets my creative juices flowing.

We've just taped Season 8 of the cooking show, *Who's Coming For Dinner*. It's rewarding to think back to the beginning and then to see how far we've come. I'm really gratified when people take the time to contact me about the show, so please pass along your comments. Check the web site for recipes, the show schedule and regular updates. www.whoscomingfordinner.com

3 Guys and a Stove is currently in its 11th year in Huntsville. We continue to serve our valued local residents year round; our summer visitors tell us that we are as much a part of their tradition as opening up the cottage for the season. And we've got some exciting news! There's a new kid in the 3 Guys and a Stove family! We've opened a second location at The Village of Blue Mountain in Collingwood. The menu is the same, the staff is excited about the new venture, and our location in the village is fantastic.

It's my hope that you will use this cookbook as an inspiration to spend some quality time in the kitchen. Use your kitchen as a place to relax, to be creative, to have fun and most of all to spend time enjoying your family and friends. Cheers, Jeff!

appetizers

BRUSCHETTA

This 'toast of Italy' is a appetizer favourite around the world.

serves 6

1 baguette loaf
1-6 oz. jar sundried tomatoes in oil
2 tbsp. garlic puree (see below)
2 pinches of dried basil
1 pinch of dried oregano
6 tbsp. grated parmesan cheese

method

Preheat oven to 400°F. Slice bread in 1 1/2 inch slices. In food processor chop sundried tomatoes until you have a fine blend. Spread mixture over each slice of bread. Lightly spread garlic puree over each slice followed with a dusting of dried herbs. Toast in oven for 8 minutes being careful not to burn. Remove from oven and grate cheese on top of each slice.

garlic puree

4 cloves garlic
1/4 cup oil

Using blender add garlic and puree. Slowly pour oil while blender is running.

APPLE & PECORINO SALAD
WITH APPLE CIDER DRESSING

The flavours of Europe shine through this simple yet sophisticated salad. The slightly bitter taste of the endive plays nicely against the sweetness of apple and the salty tang of pecorino cheese. Drizzle with apple cider dressing, add a twist of grated black pepper, and enjoy this truly flavourful salad.

serves 6
2 apples, 1 red & 1 green, sliced
2 cups mixed chicory & belgium endive
1/2 cup fresh basil leaves
1 cup pecorino cheese, shaved
1/4 cup sundried cranberries

Place all ingredients into bowl and set aside.

apple cider dressing
1/2 cup apple cider
1 tbsp. sherry vinegar
4 tbsp. extra-virgin olive oil
sea salt and freshly cracked black pepper to taste

method
Mix together salad dressing ingredients and drizzle over salad.

BAKED TORTILLA WITH BLACK BEANS, CLAMS & CILANTRO SALSA

This appetizer is stacked with great taste of cilantro, the creamy texture of cheese and the earthiness of black beans.

serves 6

2-9" flour tortillas
1 can baby clams, drained
14 oz. black beans, do not drain if using canned
3 oz. Monterey jack cheese, grated
2 tbsp. fresh cilantro, chopped (may use parsley)
1 cup salsa
1 onion, chopped
1/2 cup corn (frozen, fresh or canned and drained)
2 cloves garlic, smashed
2-3 tbsp. oil
1 tsp. cumin
1/2 cup lettuce, shredded
1/2 tbsp. crushed red chilies
2-3 sprigs of cilantro or parsley for garnish

method

Preheat oven to 400°F.

Heat skillet on medium-high; add oil, garlic, and onion sautéing until onions are transparent. Add clams, beans, corn, cumin, chilies, cilantro and salsa to the onion mixture; cook until heated through and slightly thickened. Add chopped cilantro and stir.

Spray the bottom of an ovenproof dish. Lay one tortilla in the dish, spoon half of the bean mixture over the tortilla, sprinkle half the cheese over the top of bean mixture. Repeat the same process for the second layer. Bake 10-15 minutes or until cheese melts. Garnish with parsley sprigs and shredded lettuce.

BEAN SALAD WITH LIMA BEANS, CILANTRO & PINE NUTS

The flavour of this bean salad catapults it to heights well above most bean salad recipes. Jeff's combination of buttery lima beans, green and yellow beans and turtle beans is a unique marriage of flavours. The pine nuts add texture and crunch and the aromatic cilantro adds a touch of piquancy.

serves 6

6 oz. fresh green beans
6 oz. fresh yellow beans
6 oz. lima beans, pre-cook or canned, drained
6 oz. turtle beans (commonly known as black beans), pre-cook or canned, drained
1 large handful of cilantro, chopped
2 tbsp. seasoned rice vinegar
2 tbsp. roasted pine nuts
sea salt and freshly cracked black pepper to taste

Blanch the yellow and green beans. Bring water to a boil in a saucepan. Add 1 teaspoon of salt per litre or quart of water. Plunge the green & yellow beans into the boiling water. Cook 3-5 minutes. Have a big bowl of ice-cold water ready. Strain the beans in a colander so that hot water drains into a sink. Immediately put the beans in the ice-cold water. Strain the beans as soon as they are cold. Set aside.

Roast the pine nuts. Preheat oven to 350°F. Place shelled nuts in a shallow baking pan. 'Roast' 10-20 minutes or until they are golden brown, stirring occasionally. Sprinkle sea salt to taste. Roasting improves the depth and flavour of nuts. The idea is to 'brown but not burn'. Set aside.

method

Mix all together in a bowl. Cover and set in fridge 1-2 hours for flavours to blend.

BROCCOLI & OLIVE SALAD
WITH LEMON DILL VINAIGRETTE

This colourful and healthy salad offers 'bunches of crunches.' A sprinkling of aromatic dill and zesty citrus vinaigrette and a topping of snow-white feta cheese results in a salad that's fresh tasting and delicious.

serves 4

salad ingredients
2 cups broccoli flowerets
4 cups mixed salad greens
1/2 sweet red pepper, cut into strips
1/2 sweet yellow pepper, cut into strips
1/2 cup kalamata olives, pitted

lemon dill vinaigrette ingredients
2 tbsp. extra virgin olive oil
1 tsp. lemon zest
1 tbsp. lemon juice
1 tbsp. grapefruit juice
1/2 tbsp. chopped fresh dill (a pinch if using dried dill weed)
1-2 cloves garlic, minced
pinch of red chili peppers
1 tbsp. cilantro, chopped
sea salt and freshly cracked black pepper to taste
2 oz. feta cheese, crumbled

method
Place broccoli flowerets, & a little water in a saucepan; cover with a lid and cook 1-2 minutes, shock with ice cold water then drain. It is important to keep broccoli bright green and crisp. In a big bowl, put peppers, olives, drained broccoli and mixed greens.

In a deep mixing bowl put lemon zest, lemon juice, grapefruit juice, dill, garlic, crushed red peppers, cilantro, salt and black pepper. Vigorously whisk as you pour in the oil. Pour vinaigrette over salad tossing lightly to coat. Sprinkle with feta cheese.

There are many variations of salad greens. Try one you've never used or rely on your favourites. Other vegetables that are good with this salad are sliced red onions and/or grape tomatoes. Jeff prefers feta made from sheep's or goat's milk.

CHICKEN MEXICAN HORNS WITH LIME YOGURT AND TOMATO SALSA

Hola mis amigos! You can toot your own horn when you make these Chicken Mexican Horns. They're stuffed with onions, sweet peppers, and cheese and wrapped up tight to hold in all the goodness. Topped with salsa, this dish is magnifico!

serves 4

4 whole wheat tortillas
2-4oz. chicken breast, diced
1/2 tbsp. olive oil
2 cloves garlic, minced
1 tsp. cumin
1/2 tsp. dried chilies
1/2 cup red onion, diced small
1/2 cup sweet red peppers, diced small
1/2 cup Monterey jack cheese, shredded
1/2 cup cheddar cheese, shredded
1/2 cup salsa, hot or medium
1/4 cup cilantro, chopped
sea salt and freshly cracked black pepper to taste

lime yogurt

1/4 cup plain yogurt
juice of one lime
cracked black pepper

Mix together; set aside.

method

Preheat oven to 375°F. Heat a skillet to medium-high, add olive oil and pan-sear chicken, chilies, salt and pepper for 1 minute. Add red onion, red pepper, garlic and cumin; sauté 2-3 minutes or until onion becomes translucent. Remove skillet from heat, pour contents in a bowl. Add cheeses, 1/4 cup of the salsa, cilantro and mix ingredients all together. Allow mixture to cool slightly, approximately five minutes. Cut each tortilla into thirds.

Fill tortillas with mixture and roll into a 'horn'. 'Pinch' the tiny end and put each horn seam side down in an ovenproof skillet. Bake until chicken is cooked through. Prepare lime yogurt while horns are in the oven. Serve horns with lime yogurt and remaining salsa.

FIESTA CORNBREAD

You are livin' and lovin' the flavours of the southwest whenever you eat cornbread. Jeff livens up his version with a little jalapeño and chili pepper. With the addition of cheese and creamed corn, it's yummy from the first to the last bite. It's a perfect accompaniment to Jeff's Cajun Chicken & Smoked Sausage Gumbo with Rice.

serves 6

1 cup all purpose flour
2 cups corn meal
4 tbsp. baking powder
1/2 tsp. salt
2 tbsp. sugar
1 1/2 cups Monterey jack cheese, shredded
1 can creamed corn
1 green jalapeño, remove seeds & finely dice
1 small red chili, remove seeds & finely dice
1 cup milk
2 eggs, beaten
1/4 cup olive oil

method

Preheat oven to 350°F.

In a large bowl whisk 2 eggs. Add milk, cheese, red chilies, green jalapeño, sugar, baking powder, flour, cornmeal, salt, cream corn and oil. Stir until thoroughly blended.

Pour in baking dish. Bake 25-35 minutes or until slightly brown and the center springs back to the touch.

FRESH PEI MUSSELS
WITH CURRIED COCONUT MILK

Do you order mussels when dining out, but don't make them at home? This recipe may change your mind. Mussels are fast becoming one of North America's most popular seafood due to their great versatility. This recipe has both an enticing aroma and an unforgettable taste, so give it a try.

serves 6

4 lb. raw, in-shell mussels
1/4 of a whole fresh pineapple, sliced into strips
4 tbsp. yellow curry powder
4 cups fish or vegetable stock (store bought)
1 cup light coconut milk
2 large carrots, sliced into strips
2 celery stalks, sliced into strips
1 bundle green onions, sliced into strips

method

Clean mussels by scrubbing under cold running water washing them several times and removing the beards, if present. Remember to discard any mussels with broken shells and any mussels that don't close when given a squeeze. In a large stockpot, whisk together and bring the coconut milk, vegetable stock and curry to a simmer.

Add vegetables, pineapple and simmer for 2 minutes. Add mussels. Cover and cook 2 more minutes or until the mussel shells begin to open.

Serve immediately.

GRILLED AVOCADO & ROASTED JALAPEÑO SALAD

This dish delivers auténtico south of the border flavour with ingredients found at the local grocery store. This tasty salad has many of the same ingredients as guacamole and the dressing gives it an extra helping of fiesta flare.

serves 4

2 avocados
2 jalapeño peppers, cut length-wise into quarters, remove seeds and membrane
2 tomatoes, wedges
1 clove garlic, minced
1/2 cup red onion, diced
2 tbsp. red wine vinegar
2 tbsp. extra virgin olive oil
3 tbsp. cilantro leaves, loosely chopped

fresh ginger and cumin dressing

juice from 2 limes
2 small garlic cloves, minced
1 medium jalapeño chili, minced (about 1 tbsp.)
1 tsp. cumin
1/2 tsp. fresh ginger, grated
1 tbsp. chives, chopped
1 tsp. grated orange zest
1/4 cup extra virgin olive oil
freshly cracked black pepper to taste

Mix the ginger and cumin dressing and set aside.

method

Preheat oven to 425°F. Leaving the skin on the avocados, slice in half length-wise, remove pit, and grill on the top of the stove, flesh side down with the jalapeños.

In a bowl mix together tomato, garlic, onion, vinegar and olive oil, set aside.

To serve: place grilled avocado and jalapeño slices on a plate. Spoon the tomato mixture over the avocado and jalapeño. Pour ginger and cumin dressing on top. Garnish with cilantro. Serve this salad with Jeff's Chicken Mexican Horns & Lime Yogurt.

GRILLED PINEAPPLE & MIXED GREENS WITH SHAVED COCONUT

Not just another pretty dish, this salad can stand on its own flavour. It really shows off when served with Jeff's Salmon Wrapped in Lime and Coconut Pancakes. The sweet pineapple, tasty toasted coconut, tangy watercress, and sweet papaya is a dynamic flavour combination.

serves 6
2 cups watercress
6 pineapple slices
1/2 cup shaved fresh coconut
6 slices papaya
3 cups mixed greens

red curry dressing
1 tbsp. red curry paste
4 oz. coconut milk
1 tbsp. lime juice
1 tbsp. brown sugar
2 tbsp. chopped cilantro
sea salt and freshly cracked black pepper to taste

Mix all ingredients together, stir and set aside.

method
Grill the pineapple and papaya in a cast iron grill pan, or cast iron skillet and set aside. Depending on the size of the skillet, brown the coconut shavings at the same time. A second option is to brown coconut in a preheated oven of 400°F until golden brown. Combine mixed greens, watercress, grilled pineapple & papaya; sprinkle the golden browned shaved coconut over the greens. Drizzle the dressing over the salad.

LIME MARINATED ARTICHOKE SALAD

Composing a salad of spinach, artichoke hearts, zucchini and feta cheese is a flavourful inspiration. Then, Jeff introduces the lime and cumin dressing showstopper, which takes the taste right over the top!

serves 6
3 cans artichoke hearts, drained
2 zucchini, sliced
1 cup spinach leaves, washed and dried
6-1oz. slices of feta cheese
cracked black pepper to taste

lime cumin dressing
juice from 2 limes
2 small garlic cloves, minced
1 medium jalapeño chili, minced (about 1 tbsp.)
1 tsp. cumin
1 tbsp. chives, chopped
1 tsp. grated orange zest
1/4 cup extra virgin olive oil
cracked black pepper to taste

Mix all ingredients, stir and set aside.

method
Prepare the lime cumin dressing.

Place spinach on salad plates, layer on the artichoke hearts, zucchini slices, freshly cracked pepper and feta cheese.

Spoon dressing over salad plates.

ZUCCHINI PANCAKES
WITH BAKED BRIE & MIXED BITTER GREENS

Zucchini pancake ribbons meet the mild butter and mushroom flavour of velvety brie cheese in each bite. It gets even better with the addition of crisp mixed greens and apple slices. Complete the taste with drizzle of a zippy lime and honey dressing.

serves 4
1 1/2 cups grated zucchini
2 eggs, lightly whisked
1 tbsp. melted butter combined with 1 tbsp. oil
3/4 cup flour
3/4 cup milk
1/2 tsp. grated nutmeg
6 1/2 oz. brie cheese
1 tbsp. fresh squeezed lime juice
1 tbsp. cider vinegar
2 tbsp. honey
1 small apple, cored & sliced, sprinkled with a little extra lime juice
4 cups of mixed bitter greens, washed and dried (try chicory, raddichio, & endive)
sea salt and freshly cracked black pepper to taste

method
Preheat oven to 400°F. To make pancake batter, whisk eggs & flour, stir in milk. Add zucchini, salt, pepper, and nutmeg. Stir until smooth. Heat a non-stick skillet over medium heat, add butter/oil combination. Place a large spoonful of mixture into the skillet and cook for 2 minutes on each side or until pancakes are golden. Keep pancakes warm while you continue to cook all the mixture. Put the brie in an ovenproof dish and warm in the oven, just to remove the chill, but not lose its' shape. Make the salad dressing by whisking the lime juice, vinegar, and honey. Set aside.

Cut the pancakes into strips. Remove brie from oven. Put the greens into a mixing bowl, toss with the dressing, and sliced apples. Place equal portions of greens onto four salad plates or in glass salad bowls. Top salad greens with equal strips of pancake strips. Cut the brie into 8 slices, placing 2 slices over each salad.

MEDITERRANEAN VEGETABLE SALAD

This colourful and robust salad encompasses the best characteristics of the Mediterranean. Fresh vegetables, olive oil, and black olives abound. It's like bringing a bit of the Greek islands into your kitchen.

serves 4
1 onion, sliced
2 red peppers, sliced
2 yellow peppers, sliced
2 zucchini, sliced
2 garlic cloves, minced
1/4 cup black olives, sliced
1 tbsp. fresh basil & oregano* (see note if you substitute dried herbs for fresh)
sea salt and freshly cracked black pepper to taste

dressing
1 tbsp. balsamic vinegar
3 tbsp. olive oil

method
In a big bowl, place cut vegetables, olives, garlic, fresh herbs, salt and pepper.

In a separate bowl whisk together the oil and balsamic vinegar and pour over the vegetable mixture. Toss to coat.

*Essential oils are more concentrated in dried herbs so you use less. When substituting dried herbs for fresh use this easy formula; one teaspoon dried leaves for every tablespoon of the fresh herb finely chopped.

NOODLE SALAD WITH SOY DRESSING

Jeff's salad creation has crunch and texture thanks to loads of fresh veggies. Walnut oil offers a nuttiness that complements the salty-tasting soy and rich balsamic vinegar. Add a squeeze of lime, sprinkle with icing sugar and toss in some red chilies to watch the noodles spring to life!

serves 4

1 cup rice noodles, cooked, shocked & drained
1 cup white radish,* julienned (use red if white is not available)
1 English cucumber, finely julienned
1 cup watercress, (wash & dry if necessary)

soy dressing

2 tsp. walnut oil**
1/3 cup soy sauce
1 tbsp. balsamic vinegar
4 tbsp. icing sugar
1 lime, squeezed for juice
1/2 tbsp. dried red chilies (or to taste)

Mix and set aside.

method

Bring water to boil, add salt, add noodles; boil until noodles are cooked. Drain into a colander, shock with cold water and drain again. While noodles are draining and cooling, chop radish and cucumbers into long thin strips. Place watercress, cucumber, radish and noodles into a salad bowl. Pour the dressing and toss. Serve.

*A white radish is also known as a Daikon or Japanese radish. It has a mild flavour and great crunch.

**Using walnut oil adds another dimension to this salad with its subtle yet nutty flavour. To prevent rancidity, store walnut oil in the refrigerator after opening.

ROSTI POTATO PATTIES WITH BLUE CHEESE CREAM AND LOUISIANA SAUCE

This tasty potato recipe infuses a popular Swiss staple with a little bit of Cajun excitement.

serves 4
4 whole potatoes, peeled
2 tsp. charmoula (see below)
1/4 cup blue cheese cream (see below)
1/4 cup Louisiana sauce (see below)
2 tbsp. canola oil, for frying rosti

method
Put enough water in a stockpot to cover the potatoes. Boil the potatoes. Drain and put in refrigerator until completely cooled. While potatoes are chilling prepare charmoula, blue cheese cream and Louisiana sauce.

charmoula
6 tbsp. garlic
2 tsp. cumin
2 tsp. paprika
1 tsp. sea salt
1/2 tsp. cayenne
1/2 tsp. freshly cracked black pepper
1 cup fresh chopped parsley
1/2 cup fresh chopped cilantro
6 tbsp. fresh lemon juice
4 tbsp. olive oil

Blend all ingredients in food processor. Whirl until mixture becomes a sauce like-consistency. This batch makes 2/3 cup or 6 oz.
*See suggestions on leftover portion.

blue cheese cream
1/4 cup plain yogurt
2 tbsp. crumbled blue cheese
1 1/2 tsp. dried basil
1/2 tsp. dried oregano
sea salt and freshly cracked
    black pepper, to taste

Put all ingredients in a bowl and stir vigorously until the blue cheese has blended into the yogurt. Set aside.

Louisiana sauce
5 tbsp. ketchup
1 tbsp. Cajun seasoning
    (store bought)
1 tsp. worcestershire sauce
1/2 tsp. Pommery mustard
    (or a grainy dijon)
Pinch of dried oregano
2 pinches of dried basil

Whisk all ingredients in a small bowl. Set aside.

back to the rosti
Remove cooled potatoes from the refrigerator. With your hands, mash potatoes in a large bowl. Add 2 tbsp. of the charmoula. Salt and pepper to taste. Form into patties of the desired size. The patties can be tall and skinny or flat and wide like a pancake. Heat heavy skillet to medium-high; add oil. Gently put patties into the skillet. Fry on first side; carefully turn over to the second side and fry until browned and heated through.

To serve: Put one tbsp. of the blue cheese cream on each of the four serving plates. Put one tablespoon of the Louisiana sauce beside the blue cheese cream. Evenly divide the rosti patties and put them on top of both sauces.

*Pop the unused portion of charmoula into ice cube trays. Once frozen, pop the charmoula cubes out of the tray and store in a freezer bag in the freezer. Charmoula cubes are an easy way to add flavour to soups, stews, casseroles, meat dishes, gravy, and pasta and rice dishes.

RED BEAN AND WALNUT SALAD
WITH FRESH GARLIC VINAIGRETTE

Go colour, go crunch, go fibre, and go flavour with Jeff's version of the bean salad. It's perfect for picnics or as a prelude to any meal. Walnuts add a great new dimension to this simple and tasty bean salad.

serves 4
1 can (19 oz./540 ml) red kidney beans, rinsed and drained well
1/4 cup California walnuts*, coarsely chopped

vinaigrette
2 tbsp. red onion, minced fine
1 clove garlic, minced
2 tbsp. fresh parsley, chopped
pinch of cayenne
1/4 tsp fresh cilantro, chopped
3 tbsp. red wine vinegar
1 1/2 tbsp. olive oil
sea salt to taste
cilantro for garnish (or flat-leaf parsley, if preferred)

method
Place beans and walnuts in a bowl and set aside. In a separate bowl add all the vinaigrette ingredients and whisk together. Pour over the bean mixture and toss well to coat. Garnish with fresh cilantro or parsley.

*Jeff likes to use California walnuts for their superior flavour, freshness, size and colour.

ROASTED PEAR, PECAN & SPINACH SALAD WITH HONEY MUSTARD VINAIGRETTE

The colours are vibrant in this salad. Toss tender spinach with crunchy pecans, tart cranberries, onions, peppers, honey-roasted pears, and sweet apricots and add a kick of dijon mustard and balsamic vinegar. It's a visual treat that your taste buds will love too!

serves 4
6 cups baby spinach, washed and dried
1 cup red onion, sliced
1 cup sweet yellow pepper, sliced
1/2 cup pecans, roasted
1-2 pears, cored & sliced
1 tbsp. honey

honey mustard vinaigrette
1/4 cup balsamic vinegar
2 tbsp. diced cranberries
8 dried apricots, sliced
2 tsp. dijon mustard
2 tsp. honey
3 tbsp. olive oil

Mix together and set aside until ready to use.

method
Preheat oven to 350°F.

Place pecans, pears, honey in a roasting pan and mix. Place in oven. Roast until pears turn golden brown. Remove from oven. Make honey mustard vinaigrette. Put spinach, onion, peppers in a salad bowl, add roasted pear mixture. Drizzle with the vinaigrette.

Lining roasting pan with parchment paper makes clean-up a breeze.

SESAME CHICKEN SKEWERS WITH BAKED MAPLE APPLE CHUTNEY

Open sesame! The nutty flavour of chicken and the rich, sweet taste of chutney makes this finger food tempting and delicious.

serves 6

3-4 oz. chicken breasts, boneless and skinless
1 cup sesame seeds
2 tbsp. canola oil

apple chutney sauce

1 tbsp. butter
1/4 cup maple syrup
3 apples, cored and chopped

Heat a skillet on medium-high, add 2 tbsp. oil, butter and apples and fry until softened and lightly browned; add maple syrup and reduce by half. Remove from heat, set aside.

method

Preheat oven to 400°F. Pound each chicken breast to flatten. Cut chicken into strips 1/4 inch thick coat with sesame seeds. Heat skillet to medium-high, add oil and sauté chicken 1 1/2 minutes on each side. Place skillet in oven and bake until cooked through. Serve the chicken skewers with the apple chutney sauce.

RUBBED SHRIMP WITH RAISIN, DATE & PEAR CHUTNEY

Preparing this shrimp dish can be broken down into four easy steps: clean, mix, toss and sauté...voila! Delicious shrimp jumps into a new category of flavour when you serve them with raisin, date & pear chutney. If you have never eaten shrimp prepared like this, it's time to give it a try!

serves 6
2 tbsp. paprika
2 tbsp. freshly cracked black pepper
2 tbsp. sea salt
1 tbsp. chili powder
2 tsp. brown sugar
pinch cayenne

Mix together the above rub ingredients, set aside.

24 shrimp with shells (21-25 count)
2 tbsp. oil

method
Remove shells from shrimp, leaving the tail intact; discard shells. Butterfly the shrimp (see below). Toss shrimp thoroughly to coat with the mixed spices. Heat a heavy skillet on medium high, add oil and sauté the rub-seasoned shrimp for 2-3 minutes or until done and opaque in colour. Shrimp cooks quickly so be careful not to overcook or they will become rubbery.

raisin, date & pear chutney
2 cups peeled, sliced, firm, ripe pears
1/8 cup finely chopped sweet red peppers
1/2 cup sweet onion, chopped
    (Vidalia or other sweet variety)
1/3 cup seedless raisins
1 cup sugar
1/4 cup chopped crystallized ginger
3/4 cups cider vinegar
1/8 tsp. salt
1/8 tsp. ground allspice
1/8 tsp. ground cloves
1 cinnamon stick, grated to make a 1/2 tsp.

method
Place the ingredients into a heavy saucepan on medium heat, stirring to mix thoroughly. Reduce heat and cook slowly until pears are tender and mixture thickens, about 1 hour.

how to butterfly shrimp
Cut the shrimp 3/4 open lengthwise, being careful not to cut in half. Lay the shrimp flat on a cutting board following the outside curve of the shrimp with a paring knife, cutting halfway into the body of the shrimp. Open up the shrimp, rinse under cool running water and remove the black vein. Lay shrimp on paper towel to remove excess moisture.

SPINACH SALAD WITH FAVA BEANS & ROASTED SWEET PEPPERS AND SUNDRIED CRANBERRY VINAIGRETTE

The fava bean is a staple in Mediterranean and Middle Eastern dishes so it's perfect with fresh spinach and roasted red peppers. Drizzled with cranberry vinaigrette this exotic dish also displays its Muskoka roots.

serves 6

salad ingredients
6 cups baby spinach
1/2 cup dried fava beans

sundried cranberry vinaigrette
2 oz. dried cranberries
1 oz. cranberry juice
1/2 oz. fresh lime juice
2 oz. cranberry vinegar

Combine all ingredients and whisk. Set aside.

roasted sweet peppers
4 peppers (1 red, 1 orange, 1 yellow, & 1 green - halved and seeded)
1 tbsp. oil
1 crushed garlic clove
pinch of dried basil and oregano

Set oven to 500°F. Place heavy pan in oven to heat up. Halve and remove membrane and seeds from peppers. Slice into 1 inch strips. Mix together the peppers, oil, garlic and herbs. Using an oven mitt, remove hot pan from oven. Place peppers in hot pan and return to oven to roast for about 15 minutes. Set aside.

method
Put fava beans in 2 cups of salted water, cover and cook on medium heat until soft, add more water if necessary. When cooked, remove from pan and cool. Can be done the day before and stored in fridge. Wash and dry baby spinach. Arrange spinach on 6 plates; divide the fava beans and place on top of spinach bed, spread out the roasted peppers over the spinach. Spoon the sundried cranberry vinaigrette over each plate.

SWEET POTATO CAKES WITH GEORGIA PECANS

These deep orange sweet potato and pecan cakes march to the front of the flavour and crunch line. Relish ingredients, especially the mango, red onion, and lime lead the team to first place at any meal. This special dish is a declared the victor in any versatility, taste and nutrition stakes.

serves 4

cake mixture

1 cup cooked sweet potato
1/3 cup red onion, diced
2 tbsp. fresh parsley, chopped
1/4 cup dates, finely chopped
3/4 tsp. black pepper
1 tsp. coriander
1 tsp. cumin
2 1/2 tsp. sugar
3/4 tsp. salt
1 tbsp. fresh lemon (or lime juice)

1 cup pecans, crushed for coating
1 tbsp. pumpkin seed oil and 1 tbsp. canola oil for frying

red onion mango lime relish

2 mangos, peeled & diced
1 small yellow pepper, diced
1 small red pepper, diced
1 small red onion, diced
1/2 cup mango juice
4 tbsp. lemon juice (or lime)
1 clove garlic, minced
4 tbsp. red wine vinegar
1 tbsp. curry powder

method

Put mango and lemon juice, garlic, red wine vinegar and curry powder in a bowl, stir to mix. Add peppers, onion and mango. Mixture will keep in the refrigerator for three days.

Put all cake ingredients in a bowl; mix together. Make each cake with 2 tbsp. of mixture. Roll cakes in the crushed pecans. Heat heavy skillet to medium, add both the pumpkin seed oil and canola oil and sauté each cake on both sides over medium-low heat. Serve with red onion mango lime relish.

WARM LENTIL SALAD WITH SOUR ONION JALAPEÑO SALSA

One look at this salad and you can almost taste it. But don't stop there. Making it is a big part of the experience. It's full of colour and texture and flavour that pops, thanks to cocktail onions and the peppery snap of fresh watercress.

serves 4

4 tsp. whole grain mustard
1/4 tsp. olive oil
1 tbsp. of red wine vinegar
1 cup lentils, (1/2 red, 1/2 yellow), cooked*
1/2 red onion, chopped
1 tsp. fresh tarragon, chopped
1 tsp. fresh sage, chopped
1 tsp. fresh parsley, chopped
4 cups watercress
sea salt and freshly cracked black pepper to taste

sour onion jalapeño salsa

1/2 cup sour cocktail onions
1/2 jalapeño, chopped
1/3 cup cilantro, chopped
1/2 -1 tsp. chipotle sauce (brands vary in intensity)

Combine salsa ingredients in a bowl and mix. Set aside.

method

Cook lentils and set aside. Make sour onion jalapeño salsa, set aside. In a bowl, whisk mustard, olive oil and red vinegar. Pour over the warm lentils; add the onions, herbs, salt and pepper. Serve lentils over a bed of watercress. Spoon sour onion jalapeño salsa over the lentils.

cooking lentils

Rinse and drain. Cover with water or vegetable broth and boil for 2 to 3 minutes (to aid in digestion). Reduce heat and simmer until tender. Do not add salt in the cooking process, this can toughen the lentils.

*1 cup dry lentils = 2 to 2 1/2 cups cooked.

Cannot find fresh tarragon or sage? Use dried. A general rule of thumb in converting fresh to dry is to use about half as much dried as fresh herbs. Dried parsley offers no flavour but the good news is that fresh parsley is available year-round. Flat leaf or Italian parsley has the most intense flavour. Jalapeño: Most of the heat in a jalapeño is actually contained in the membrane. Rubber gloves can be worn to protect hands and eyes.

SPIDER SHRIMP WITH REDNECK HOT SAUCE

This dish is a little bit country and a little bit …a work of art. It's a showstopper at dinner parties; your guests will definitely want to know how you did it.

serves 4

12 shrimp [21-25 count], peeled deveined and butterflied
2 cups cooked spaghetti, cooled
oil for deep frying
1/4 cup redneck hot sauce
12 slices of lemon

redneck hot sauce

1 tbsp. Cajun seasoning (Jeff likes to use Lawrey's)
1 tsp. water
4 tbsp. ketchup
1 tbsp. vinegar
1/2 tbsp. Pommery mustard (may substitute Dijon or Creole mustard)
1/2 tbsp. herb mix (2 parts basil, 1 part oregano)
1/4 tbsp. worcestershire sauce

Put all ingredients into a bowl and whisk until thoroughly combined.

method

Prepare redneck sauce. Heat oil in deep fryer until it reaches 375°F. Wrap 5-6 strands of spaghetti around each piece of shrimp.

Gently place shrimp into fryer; cook two minutes. The shrimp will cook quickly and the spaghetti will crisp. Carefully remove shrimp from hot oil, using tongs. Add cooked shrimp to the redneck sauce and gently toss to cover shrimp. Serve immediately with lemon.

WATERCRESS, KALAMATA OLIVE & GREEN ONION SALAD WITH GOAT CHEESE DRESSING

Crisp green watercress is delightful when paired with the meaty flavour of kalamata olives. The goat cheese dressing combines smooth buttermilk and goat cheese blended with Dijon mustard, garlic, lemon zest, and fresh herbs to make a super-star salad.

serves 4
4-5 cups watercress*, washed and dried
16 kalamata olives, pitted
3-4 green onions, sliced into thin strips

Mix in salad bowl. Set aside.

goat cheese dressing
4 oz. fresh goat cheese, room temperature
1/4 cup buttermilk
1 clove garlic, minced
3 tsp. white wine vinegar
2 tsp. dijon mustard
1 tsp. fresh thyme, minced
1 tsp. fresh parsley, minced
1 tbsp. fresh chives
1-2 tsp. grated lemon zest
sea salt to taste
fresh cracked black pepper to taste

method
Prepare goat cheese dressing. Whisk all ingredients in a bowl. If the mixture is too thick, thin with additional buttermilk. Adjust seasonings if desired. It is ready to use or cover and refrigerate for later use. Makes 1 cup. Save extra dressing for later use. Pour enough dressing over salad to lightly coat greens. Serve.

*Substitute arugula, spinach, or your favourite greens mix.

CORN & CHEESE TART

These savory nibbles bring a bit of the bistro to brunch or dinner. The ingredients create a wonderful blend of flavour. These tarts are served at 3 Guys and a Stove every weekend with our breakfast plate and are served with corn fried tomatoes.

makes 16 tarts

1/2 cup corn (fresh, frozen or canned)
1/2 cup shredded jack cheese
1/2 cup diced tomatoes
1/4 cup diced onions
2 tbsp. salsa
1/4 cup feta cheese, crumbled
1/4 cup canned black beans, rinsed & drained
16 unsweetened tart shells (store bought)

method

Preheat oven to 350°F. In a large bowl mix first seven ingredients together. Fill each tart shell with one heaping tbsp. of filling.

Place filled tarts on a baking sheet and bake approximately 15 minutes or until filling is set and cheese starts to bubble. Remove from oven. Cool tarts on rack for 10 minutes. Serve warm or at room temperature.

CALAMARI

Sizzlin' with flavour, calamari has the sweet, mild taste of the ocean. It's a delicacy that can easily be enjoyed at home, so don't wait to visit a restaurant. Dust each calamari ring with aromatic tandoori spices and pan-fry quickly. Serve with sesame seed dipping sauce.

serves 6
1 1/2 cup calamari tubes, cut into 1/8 inch rings
3/4 cup sesame glaze
2 limes, cut in half
2 cups calamari flour
oil for deep frying

calamari flour
2 cups whole wheat flour
3 level tbsp. tandoori spice (you can buy this at your local grocery store)

Place ingredients in bowl and mix.

sesame seed glaze
1-19 oz. can pumpkin puree
1 onion, minced
3 cloves garlic, minced
2 oz. sesame oil
5 tbsp. sesame seeds
1/2 cup water
1/2 cup soya
5 tbsp. rice vinegar

tandoori spice recipe
4 tsp. curry
1 tsp. ginger
1/4 tsp. cinnamon
1/4 tsp. garlic powder
1/2 tsp. cumin
1/2 tsp. salt
2 tsp. paprika

Place ingredients in bowl and mix.

method
Add oil to sauce pan, add onions and garlic then sauté. Add pumpkin, soya, water, rice vinegar and sesame seeds. Cook on medium heat, stirring constantly. Cook for 45 minutes to 1 hour. Do not boil. Refrigerate and cool. Once cooled add 3 tbsp. of sesame oil to shine/add gloss.

method
Add calamari to calamari flour mixture. Mix and dust off excess flour from the calamari rings. Fry calamari in oil at 325°F for 2 minutes. Remove calamari from oil and serve with sesame seed glaze. Heat limes in the microwave for 20 seconds and squeeze lime juice over the calamari.

Ensure that calamari is floating in the oil when cooking. Whole wheat flour is preferable to white flour because the whole wheat flour is more dense; it protects the calamari from overcooking and allows the product to be crisp on the outside.

LENTIL SOUP WITH ROASTED ALMONDS

This highly-flavoured vegetarian soup is brimming with vegetables and good taste. Salted almonds to this dish add a touch of crunch.

serves 6

2-3 tbsp. olive oil
6 cloves garlic, minced
1 Spanish sweet onion, diced
1/2 tsp. dried oregano
1 1/2 tsp. dried basil
1/4 cup sweet red pepper, diced
1/4 cup rutabaga, diced
1/4 cup carrot, diced
1 cup of lentils, any colour, pre-soaked
7 cups vegetable stock (good quality available in tetra packs in grocery stores, preferably without MSG)
freshly cracked black pepper to taste

12-1 inch long x 1/8 inch thick rutabaga sticks
12-1 inch long x 1/8 inch thick carrot sticks
6 tsp. salted almonds (store bought)

method

Heat a soup pot to medium-high. Add 2 1/2 tbsp. oil, garlic, onions, oregano, basil, red peppers, diced rutabaga and diced carrot. Sauté until onions are translucent. Add soaked, drained lentils and vegetable stock and cook over medium heat approximately 45 minutes to one hour. Add freshly cracked black pepper.

Heat a small skillet to medium-high. Add 1/2 tbsp. of oil, the 12 carrots and rutabaga sticks and sear quickly until lightly browned but not too soft. Garnish each bowl of soup with 1 tbsp. salted almonds, 2 rutabaga sticks, and 2 carrot sticks.

CREAM OF POTATO & SMOKED SALMON SOUP

This creamy, smoky salmon flavoured soup is the perfect introduction to dinner. If you ladle a little more into the bowl and add a crusty piece of bread, this wonderfully satisfying soup becomes an entire meal. Nothing beats a steaming hot bowl of soup!

serves 6

3 medium potatoes, cut into thin strips, 1 inch long
4 tbsp. olive oil
1/4 cup sliced leeks
2 green onions, sliced
6 cups vegetable stock
2 tbsp. worcestershire sauce
1/2 tsp. dried oregano
1 1/2 tsp. dried basil
6 oz. smoked salmon, finely sliced and cut into strips
sea salt and freshly cracked black pepper to taste

1 tbsp. capers, optional
2 tbsp. chopped dill for garnish

vegetable velouté

7 cups vegetable stock (good quality available in tetra packs in grocery stores, preferably without MSG)
1 cup all purpose flour

Pour cold stock into a large saucepan reserving a 1/2 cup of the stock and bring to a boil. Using the 1/2 cup of the stock, whisk the flour into the cold stock until it is absolutely smooth. Take the flour mixture and pour slowly into the hot stock, stirring constantly. Reduce to simmer as velouté thickens in approximately 10 minutes.

method

Make velouté. Set aside. Heat a soup pot to medium-high. Add oil, leeks, green onion, oregano, basil, potato and sauté until the leeks and potatoes soften. Add the volute and bring mixture to a simmer. Add worcestershire sauce and continue simmering on low for approximately 30 minutes or until potatoes are tender and cooked.

Divide the salmon into 6 soup bowls, add 3-4 capers over the salmon and pour in the hot soup. Taste and adjust seasoning if desired. To garnish, sprinkle dill over the soup.

NAVAJO FLAT BREAD WITH GOAT CHEESE, RICOTTA, BLACK OLIVES & ROASTED GARLIC

This is a very popular appetizer at 3 Guys and a Stove. The flat bread is topped with creamy goat & ricotta cheese, sweet roasted garlic and a few black olives, to bring a little of the Southwest into your kitchen.

serves 4
4 flat breads (see recipe and method below)
1/2 cup ricotta cheese
8 tbsp. goat cheese
1/2 cup black olives, sliced
4 tbsp. garlic puree
2 tsp. dried oregano
2 tsp. dried basil
pinch of salt
2 tbsp. of olive oil to drizzle over each flatbread

flat bread dough
2 cups whole wheat flour
2 tbsp. baking powder
2 tsp. salt
3/4 cup water (add water slowly to achieve the consistency of dough)

method
Prepare flatbread dough. Mix flour, baking powder and salt in a bowl. Gradually add warm water until all the flour is mixed and the dough no longer sticks to your hands. Turn onto a floured board and knead until dough is soft. Wrap the dough in plastic wrap and allow it to rest at room temperature for 1 hour.
Make garlic puree. (See recipe below) Set aside.

Preheat oven to 425°F. Once dough has rested for one hour, cut into quarters. Roll each quarter on a floured surface into an 8-10 inch circle. Place dough on a pizza pan, pie plate or cookie sheet. On each flatbread, spread the ricotta cheese, goat cheese evenly and add black olives to each. Spoon the garlic puree over the cheeses and add olive oil evenly to each. Add herbs and salt. Bake for 20 minutes or until crust is crisp.

garlic puree
4 cloves garlic
1/4 cup oil

Using blender add garlic and puree. Slowly pour oil while blender is running.

ROASTED CHICKEN
AND WHITE BEAN BROTH

Flavourful broth soup can be made in moments using leftover chicken, canned beans and quality chicken stock. It's just what the chef ordered when time is at a premium.

serves 4

1/2 cup cooked white navy beans (wash and drain if using canned)
6 cups chicken stock (store bought)
2 tbsp. soya sauce
1 1/2 cups cooked, boneless and skinless chicken, dark, white or mixed
2 cups fresh vegetable mixture (see below)
1 1/2 tbsp. dried basil
1/2 tbsp. dried oregano
2 cloves garlic, minced
4 tbsp. canola oil
1 fresh tomato, diced

method

Heat a soup pot to medium-high. Add oil, vegetable mixture, garlic, and herbs and sauté until onion becomes translucent. Add cooked chicken, soya sauce, chicken stock, and white beans. Bring to a boil. Reduce to a simmer, add diced tomatoes and cook uncovered for 30 minutes.

ingredients for vegetable mixture (Use your favourite combination of vegetables)

- red onion, sliced thinly
- zucchini, cut into quarters lengthwise and diced
- green, red and yellow peppers, cored, cut into 1/4 inch strips and chopped
- mushrooms cut into quarters
- turnip, cut into 1/2 inch thick
- eggplant, cut into 1/2 inch slices and diced

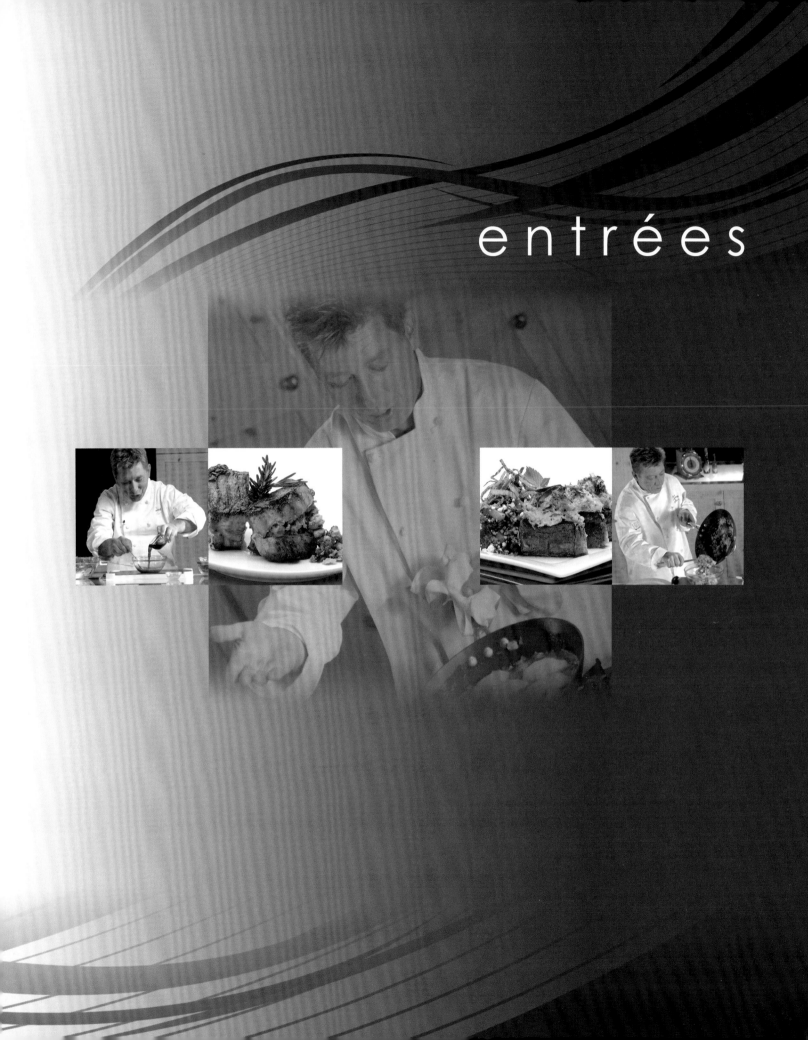

entrées

SEARED CANADIAN BEEF SHORT RIBS WITH ROASTED VEGETABLES & WHITE BEAN RAGOUT

Jeff serves the beef short ribs with a satisfying and delicious bean ragout that is 'chock full' of roasted vegetables topped off with a dab of creamy horseradish.

serves 4
12 beef short ribs
1/2 cup flour
1/3-2/3 cups olive oil
1 red onion, sliced
2 cloves garlic, minced
1 tsp. fresh rosemary leaves, strip leaves from stems
4 stalks celery, cut diagonally
4 carrots, cut diagonally
2 cups dried white beans, soaked overnight, rinsed and drained
2 cups vegetable stock (store bought)
2-3 tbsp. tomato paste
zest of 1 lemon
2 tbsp. of fresh horseradish, grated
1/4 cup Italian parsley, chopped
4 plum tomatoes, chopped
sea salt and freshly cracked black pepper to taste
store bought creamed horseradish (when serving)

method
Preheat oven to 400°F. Coat beef ribs with flour. Heat a large ovenproof pot or casserole pan to medium-high, add oil and sear to brown ribs on both sides. Add onion, garlic, rosemary, celery, and carrots and sauté until onion becomes translucent. Add horseradish, lemon zest and parsley and stir. Add beans, tomatoes and vegetable stock, stir to combine.

Cover casserole with a tight lid or foil. Bake until the meat pulls easily from the bone, at least 3 to 3 1/2 hours. Serve with store bought creamed horseradish.

BLACK SEA BASS WITH SWEET & SOUR CANDIED LIMES & RHUBARB SAUCE

Black sea bass is a great fish to cook and eat. The tender and flaky white flesh has a subtle flavor, which the sugared limes bring to life. Add a pinch of cinnamon, some rhubarb, and honey for a nice touch of sweetness. Cilantro and ginger add some complexity to the over-all flavour of the dish.

serves 6

6-6 oz. black sea bass fillets
2 limes, sliced into 3 rings per lime
4 tbsp. olive oil
1/2 cup of Spanish onion, sliced
1 cup rhubarb, cut into 1-inch pieces (if out of season, use frozen, thawed and drained)
4 tbsp. honey
1 1/4 tsp. sea salt
1 1/2 tsp. peeled and minced fresh ginger
1/4 tsp. cinnamon
1/2 cup of canned & diced tomatoes including juice
freshly cracked black pepper to taste
1 cup all purpose flour for coating fish fillets
1/4 cup chopped fresh mint, reserve several sprigs for garnish
1/4 cup white sugar to coat limes
1/4 cup cilantro, washed and chopped (if preferred use parsley)

method

Preheat oven to 425°F. Coat the sea bass fillets in flour; set aside. Heat a large skillet to medium-high; add 1-2 tbsp. oil and cook onions until they are slightly caramelized. Add tomatoes, rhubarb, honey, salt, ginger, pepper, chopped mint and cinnamon. Reduce heat to simmer.

While mixture simmers, heat a second large oven-proof skillet to medium-high; add 3 tbsp. oil and sauté fish 2 minutes on each side. Place lime slices alongside fish to gently sauté. Remove skillet from heat. Gently remove limes from skillet and coat each side of the lime slices with sugar. Pour heated rhubarb mixture over the sea bass in the skillet. Lay sugared limes on the sea bass and rhubarb mixture.

Put skillet in hot oven and cook until the flesh of the sea bass becomes opaque yet is still moist on the inside. A secret to successful sea bass cookery is not overcooking it. A good rule of thumb for cooking time is about 10 minutes per inch of thickness.

When fish is cooked remove skillet from oven. Sprinkle in cilantro. To serve, lay sea bass on warmed plate, spoon rhubarb mixture over the fish. Place 2 limes (per serving) on the sea bass and garnish with mint sprigs.

CAJUN CHICKEN &
SMOKED SAUSAGE GUMBO WITH RICE

This gumbo is straight out of the black iron pots of Louisiana! Jeff's delicious gumbo is thick Cajun soup with the flavours of chicken, sausage and vegetables blending together in a rich brown roux. Although most Cajun cooking is 'a little of this and that' Jeff's recipe takes what he learned from his exciting New Orleans cooking experience and shares it so you too can enjoy a taste of Louisiana.

serves 12

1 chicken, cut into 8 pieces (or use 8 pieces of your favourite chicken cuts)
3 smoked sausage, cut into 1 1/2" pieces
1/2 cup vegetable oil
2 cups flour
2 cups onions, diced
2 cups celery, diced
1 cup red peppers, diced
1/4 cup diced garlic
1 tbsp. thyme, dried
1/2 tsp. rosemary, dried
3 quarts chicken stock (store bought)
24 mushrooms, sliced
2 cups sliced green onions
1 cup chopped parsley
sea salt and cracked black pepper to taste
1 tsp. cayenne, optional
2 cups cooked brown rice

method

In a 2 gallon stockpot, heat 1 tbsp. oil over medium-high heat, add chicken and sausage and sear to brown. Using a slotted spoon remove all meat from the pan. Add the rest of the oil. Sprinkle in flour and using a wire whisk, stir constantly until the 'roux' is golden brown. Be careful not to scorch. Add onion, celery, green pepper, mushrooms, rosemary, cayenne and garlic and cook approximately 3 to 5 minutes or until vegetables are wilted. Add chicken and sausage to the vegetable mixture. Add chicken stock, one ladle at a time, stirring constantly until all is incorporated. Bring to a quick boil, then immediately reduce to a simmer and continue to cook approximately 30 minutes or until chicken is fully cooked. Add green onions and parsley and cook an additional 5 minutes. Season to taste. Serve with cooked brown rice.

Roux: A flour and oil mixture used to start almost all Louisiana dishes. Roux is used in many soups and sauces and is considered a staple of Cajun and Creole dishes.

Cajun cooking tends to be more 'country-style and primarily rustic' while Creole is more cosmopolitan and slightly more sophisticated. Both styles of cooking are counted as treasures of Louisiana!

CERTIFIED ANGUS TOP SIRLOIN WITH THREE MUSHROOM NOODLE RAGOUT

It's hard to resist an incredibly tender, naturally juicy steak at any time, but when you add a medley of meaty mushrooms, it's downright impossible to resist. Why would you even try?

serves 4

4-6 oz. cuts (baseball cut) of top sirloin
2 cups mixed mushrooms, sliced (button, shiitake & portobello)
2 tbsp. olive oil
1 tbsp. butter
6 oz. beef stock (store bought)
2 cups egg noodles, cooked
3 cloves garlic, crushed
1 tsp. mixed herbs (2 parts basil, 1 part oregano)
sea salt and freshly cracked black pepper to taste

method

Preheat oven to 450°F. Heat an oven proof skillet to medium high. Add oil and butter and pan sear both sides of the meat. Season with sea salt and pepper. Remove sirloin from the skillet and place into an oven proof dish and into the oven. Leave in oven for approximately 10 minutes to obtain a medium-rare cooking temperature (leave longer for if you would like it cooked more).

Using the same skillet that the sirloin was cooked in, add the mushroom assortment and sauté. Add garlic, herbs and the stock and reduce by 1/4. Add noodles, stir and serve when the noodles are hot, approximately 2 minutes.

To serve, remove the sirloin from the oven. Place the mushroom and noodle mixture onto a plate. Add the sirloin, enjoy!

FYI: internal temperature is 145°F for medium rare, 160°F for medium, and 170°F for well-done.

CHEESE RAVIOLI WITH RICOTTA, LEMON, SPINACH & BASIL

Say 'cheese' and 'pass-ta' the ravioli. Jeff's simple cheese ravioli dish bursts with flavour in every bite. As a bonus, it's easy to make. The dish is enhanced with baby spinach, cherry tomatoes, fresh basil, and creamy ricotta cheese. Grate a little fresh parmesan, load your fork, and close your eyes. It's a taste of Italy right in your own kitchen.

serves 4

1 lb. cheese filled ravioli (store bought)
12 cups vegetable stock (store bought)
2 tbsp. olive oil
1/4 cup lemon juice
1/4 cup fresh parmesan cheese
1 cup baby spinach
1/2 cup ricotta cheese
1/3 cup fresh basil leaves
sea salt and freshly cracked black pepper to taste

method

Heat vegetable stock in a saucepan, bring to a boil and add pasta. Cook quickly, drain and set aside, reserving 1/2 cup of the stock. Heat a skillet to medium-high, add oil, spinach, basil leaves, a little vegetable stock, lemon juice and sauté 1-2 minutes. Add whole cherry tomatoes, sea salt and cracked black pepper. Cook until tomatoes are heated.

Assemble by putting cooked pasta on platter, top with hot vegetables, and sprinkle with ricotta and freshly grated parmesan cheese.

SCRAMBLED EGGS AND CHUNKY TOMATO & OLIVE RELISH WITH SQUASH & POTATO CAKE

What's crackin'? Did someone say eggs for dinner? Eggs-actly… and they are eggs-traordinary with the Squash and Potato Cakes and Chunky Tomato & Olive Relish.

serves 4
potato cake
2 Yukon gold potatoes, cubed
2 cups squash, cubed (butternut is good)
1/4 red onion, diced
4 tbsp. mayonnaise
1 cup flour (can use half white and half whole wheat)
1 tsp. mixed herbs (2 parts basil, 1 part oregano)
sea salt and freshly cracked black pepper to taste
canola oil to sauté squash & potato cakes

method
Bring water in a saucepan to a boil, add potato & squash cubes. Reduce heat and simmer until vegetables are cooked. Drain in a colander and slightly cool. As potato and squash cook, prepare the olive relish, (see below), set aside. Return to the potato & squash. Mix together the potato, squash, onion, mayonnaise, flour, herbs, salt & pepper in a bowl. Form into patties. Heat a heavy skillet to medium-high; add oil and sauté potato cakes on one side. Reduce heat to medium, carefully flip to second side and continue to cook until golden brown.

herbed scrambled eggs
4 large eggs
2-3 chives, chopped fine
1/2 tbsp. canola oil

Crack eggs and chopped chives into a deep bowl and whisk until well combined. Heat a heavy skillet over medium-low. Add oil to the skillet, pour in egg mixture and allow the eggs to cook undisturbed until they begin to set. Then stir them off the bottom of the pan gently. Continue cooking until the eggs are the consistency you like.

olive relish
1/2 lemon, squeezed
1/4 cup whole green olives
1/4 cup whole black olives
1/4 cup tomato, cut into chunks
1/4 cup red onion, diced fine
1 clove garlic, minced
2 tbsp. flat leaf parsley, chopped
2 tbsp. olive oil
sea salt and cracked black pepper to taste

Mix all relish ingredients in a bowl, stir and set aside.

Place the potato squash cakes onto plate and serve with herbed scrambled eggs and olive relish on side.

JUMBO SHRIMP WITH WALNUT PESTO & GREEN TABASCO

When you combine the 'royal herb' (basil) and the 'fruit of the valley' (walnuts) with extra-virgin olive oil and pungent garlic, the result is perfect pesto. It's the only one that does justice to the jumbo shrimp know as 'ocean candy.'

serves 4

16 jumbo shrimp (16-21 count), cleaned, peeled and deveined
1/2 cup walnut pieces (use a good quality walnut)
1/4 cup fresh parsley, chopped
1/4 cup fresh basil, chopped
2 garlic cloves, minced
4 tbsp. olive oil
1/2 tbsp. butter
sea salt and freshly cracked black pepper to taste
2 oz. green tabasco sauce*

method

Devein the shrimp by making a slit along the back or outside of the shrimp. Lift out the black vein and discard. Rinse the shrimp and dry on paper towel.

Put the basil and parsley in a mortar and begin to mash with the pestle. Add garlic, sea salt and walnuts, building on the flavour before whisking in 1 tbsp. of olive oil to form a well-integrated mixture. Set aside.

Heat a large skillet to medium-high; add 2 tbsp. oil and the butter and quickly brown shrimps until they are cooked through. (Careful not to overcook or shrimps will become tough.) Transfer to a heated serving platter, spoon the pesto over the shrimps and sprinkle with the green tabasco sauce. Serve immediately.

pesto

If you would like to add parmesan cheese to this pesto, add it before the oil, mash a bit then add the oil. The product is not quite the same when you use a food processor instead of a mortar and pestle because you tend to get a pureed pesto instead of a mash. Both methods produce a delicious pesto no matter which one you use. If you are using a food processor to make the pesto, add the garlic to the food processor and mince. Next, add the basil leaves, walnuts, sea salt and pulse. (Add parmesan cheese at this point if desired.) While the processor is running, slowly drizzle in olive oil through the feed tube until all the ingredients are blended.

*Green tabasco sauce is all about the flavour of jalapeño peppers, yet it's the mildest of the tabasco family. Rich and tangy, it has a gentler heat that won't blow you away.

LAMB PICADILLO CABBAGE ROLLS

Jeff infuses his cabbage rolls with some Mexican flair by using olives, ground lamb, red chilies, cumin, and chipolte sauce instead of the usual ingredients. It elevates the humble cabbage roll to new heights of flavour.

serves 4

picadillo filling

1 lb. ground lamb
1 onion, diced
2 tsp. olive oil
2 garlic cloves, minced
1/2 cup sweet red pepper, diced
1/2 tsp. dried oregano

1 tsp. dried basil
1 tsp. cumin
1/2 cup of tomato juice
(from drained canned tomatoes)
1/4 cup raisins
1/4 cup black olives, sliced
pinch of dried red chilies

2 tbsp. red wine vinegar
1/8 tsp. cinnamon stick, grated
1 cup brown rice, cooked
8 large savoy cabbage leaves
several fresh mint leaves for garnish

method

Heat a stockpot with lightly salted water. Remove core from cabbage. Steam the cabbage for approximately 5 minutes until leaves are tender enough to separate easily without tearing. Run under cold water and drain. Cut the thick membrane off back of each leaf and set aside until ready to stuff.

Heat a large skillet on medium-high, add oil, lamb, onion, red pepper and sauté until onion becomes translucent; add garlic and dried herbs, chilies and sauté another minute. Add tomato juice, raisins, olives, red wine vinegar, and grated cinnamon, cook 5 minutes to develop flavour and thicken. Remove from heat and cool. Mix cooked rice into filling.

sauce

1/2 red onion, chopped
1/2 Spanish onion, chopped
1/2 cup sweet red peppers
1/2 tbsp. olive oil
1/4 cup parsley, chopped
1-19 oz. can plum tomatoes;
        drain and reserve juice for filling
2 tbsp. tomato paste
1 garlic clove, minced
2 tbsp. brown sugar
pinch of dried red chilies
8 dashes of chipotle sauce (store bought)

Heat a large skillet on medium-high, add oil, onions, red peppers, and sauté until onion becomes translucent. Add all other sauce ingredients and simmer 5-10 minutes.

assemble

With stem end of leaf toward you, place about 2 to 3 tablespoons of the picadillo filling width-wise along the lower end of the leaf. Roll bottom of leaf over mixture once, tuck in right and left sides of leaf, then finish rolling forward, making sure ends are all tucked in.

Place the seam side down in a roasting pan.

Pour sauce over the cabbage rolls. Cover with lid and finish in oven at 300°F for approximately 1 1/2 hours.

LOW COUNTRY TURKEY BREAST WITH FRESH CRANBERRY PEACH GLAZE

Low country cuisine hails from the American southwest coastal region. Jeff combines low country elements with northern cranberries and exotic herbs in this unique turkey recipe. The result is a modern mélange of high flavour that is spectacularly delicious.

serves 4

1 lb. turkey breast, cut into 4 oz. pieces, breaded in corn flour mixture
1 1/2 cups vegetable stock
8 oz. polenta*, sliced into 4, 1/2" thick (store bought)
2 tbsp. red onions, diced
1 tbsp. olive oil
1/2 cup white wine
1/2 cup fresh or frozen whole cranberries
1/2 cup sliced peaches

corn flour coating

1 cup corn flour
3/4 tsp. cumin
3/4 tsp. chili powder
3/4 tsp. coriander
1/4 tsp. salt
coarsely ground black pepper to taste
2 tbsp. olive oil

Mix coating ingredients in a bowl.

method

Dredge each piece of turkey with the cornflour coating. Heat a heavy skillet to medium-high, add oil and sauté turkey on both sides and continue cooking thoroughly until the juices run clear when pierced with a fork. Remove from skillet and set aside. Add onions to the skillet and sauté until they become translucent. Add white wine and cook until wine evaporates. Add cranberries, peaches and vegetable stock and continue to cook until the liquid has reduced by half. Set aside.

In a separate pan, fry polenta slices 2 minutes on each side.

Place polenta in the center of a dinner plate, add turkey on top of polenta and drizzle with the cranberry and peach glaze.

*Polenta rolls can be purchased at any grocery store. You certainly can make your own, but it is much easier to purchase. Polenta is simply made from corn meal.

PAN SEARED GROUPER WITH PINK PEPPERCORN, PICKLED GINGER & WATERMELON RELISH

Grouper has mild but distinct flavor, a cross between bass and halibut. Jeff gives it a one-two-three punch with his pink peppercorn, pickled ginger & watermelon relish. The jalapeño intensifies the flavour while the honey and watermelon sweetens it.

serves 4

4-6oz. grouper fillets
4 tbsp. olive oil
2 tbsp. fresh lime juice
2 tsp. pink peppercorns
8 slices candied ginger, chopped fine (each slice of ginger is the size of a quarter)
1/2 cup of cilantro leaves, washed and chopped
1 tbsp. lemongrass (finely chop the bulb)
2 tbsp. canola or grapeseed oil
sea salt and freshly cracked black pepper to taste
lemon & lime slices

method

Combine olive oil, lime juice, peppercorns, ginger, cilantro and lemongrass in bowl. Stir and set aside.

watermelon relish

2 cups watermelon, seeded and diced into 3/4 inch cubes
1/4 cup red onion, diced
1 jalapeño, seeded and minced
2 tsp. honey
sea salt and freshly cracked black pepper to taste
1/2 tbsp. fresh mint, chopped

Combine the watermelon, red onion, jalapeño and honey in bowl; stir and set aside.

Heat a heavy skillet to medium-high; add canola oil. Place the flesh side of the grouper down in the skillet and cook for approximately 3 minutes each side.

Place fish onto plates, spoon on the peppercorn and ginger mixture and top with the watermelon relish.

The flavours and textures of this dish go very well with Jeff's Warm Lentil Salad with Sour Onion Jalapeño Salsa.

STUFFED PORK LOIN WITH CRAWFISH & WATER CHESTNUT STUFFING

The crawfish and water chestnut stuffing gives this pork loin dish some real pizzazz!

serves 4
4-6 oz. boneless pork loin
1 cup crawfish & water chestnut stuffing (see below)
2 tbsp. olive oil
1 clove garlic, minced
1 tsp. dried basil
1/2 tsp. dried oregano
sea salt and freshly cracked black pepper to taste

crawfish & water chestnut stuffing
2 cups whole wheat bread cubes
1 tbsp. olive oil
1 cup celery, chopped
1/2 cup sweet red pepper, chopped
1/3 cup onion, chopped
8 oz. crawfish, chopped coarsely
2 tsp. Creole seasoning
1/2 cup green onion, chopped
1 can water chestnuts, drained & sliced
1 cup vegetable stock
cayenne pepper taste

method
Heat skillet to medium-high, add oil and sauté celery, red pepper and onion until onion is translucent. Add the crawfish tails, Creole seasoning and cayenne. Sauté for 3 minutes. Add the bread cubes, water chestnuts, green onion and stock. Mix well.

method
Preheat oven to 425°F. Stuff the pork chops with the crawfish stuffing being careful not to over stuff. Mix 1 tbsp. oil, garlic and dried herbs together and rub over the outside of the stuffed pork loin. Heat heavy skillet to medium-high, add 1 tbsp. of oil and carefully pan-sear the pork loins on both sides. It's important not to squeeze the chops as you turn them; you want the stuffing to stay in place.

Place skillet in oven and pan roast until pork is cooked, but not overdone. A safe internal temperature is 160°F. Remove from oven and allow the meat to relax and the juices to flow back.

LOCAL LAMB WITH
FRESH HORSERADISH & RHUBARB

Experiencing the flavour is what this lamb dish is all about. The succulent lamb medallions only get better with the zesty addition of fresh horseradish and mouth-watering rhubarb. This is a surprisingly easy to prepare dish that is as elegant as it is simple.

serves 4

16-2 oz. lamb loin medallions
3-4 tbsp. plain yogurt
1/2 tsp. dried basil
1/4 cup fresh rhubarb, shredded
1/4 cup fresh horseradish, shredded
2 tbsp. olive oil
1 clove garlic, minced
1 cup untoasted buckwheat
1/4 cup black olives
2 cups of mixed vegetables, chopped
   (onion, sweet red pepper, zucchini, mushrooms, turnip, eggplant, asparagus or your favourite mixture)
2 cups of vegetable stock (store bought)
1 tsp. dried basil
1/2 tsp. dried oregano
1/2 cup feta cheese, crumbled
fresh mint for garnish
sea salt and freshly cracked black pepper to taste

method

Set oven on broil. Blend shredded horseradish, rhubarb, yogurt, basil, salt and pepper in food processor. Set aside.

Heat a large skillet to medium-high, add oil, mixed vegetables and dried herbs; sauté until onion becomes translucent. Add buckwheat, vegetable stock and olives and cook 3-5 minutes.

While buckwheat cooks, heat a cast iron skillet on the stove to medium-high and place lamb loin in skillet. Grill 2 minutes on each side, cover with the shredded horseradish, rhubarb and yogurt mixture. Broil 2 to 3 minutes until lamb reaches desired doneness. (Jeff's personal preference is medium-rare.) If the horseradish-rhubarb coating begins to burn, move skillet with lamb to a lower rack to finish broiling. Remove lamb and allow it to rest for 5 minutes.

Place cooked vegetable-buckwheat mixture on a platter, lay lamb loins over the vegetables, sprinkle with feta cheese and garnish with fresh mint.

Cast iron distributes heat evenly, retains heat and is easy to clean. It is also compatible with standard stovetops, induction ranges, and conventional ovens.

PUMPKIN RISOTTO WITH WHITE CHEDDAR & FRESH ASPARAGUS

Arborio rice releases plenty of starch while cooking, which helps to give the dish its proper creamy texture. Risotto is all about building flavour, and this recipe ensures that the grains absorb plenty of the stock and herbs that give this risotto its lovely taste.

serves 4

1 cup arborio rice (a fat, starchy, medium grain rice)
1/2 cup pumpkin purée
1/3 cup honey
2 tsp. curry
3 1/2 cups + 1 cup vegetable stock (store bought)
1/2 tsp. dried basil
1/4 tsp. dried oregano
1 lb. asparagus, washed and cut
1 onion, diced
2 oz. white cheddar cheese, grated

method

Heat 3 1/2 cups vegetable stock in a saucepan and keep it simmering. (Note: it is important to add hot stock, not cold, to the rice during the cooking process. Adding cold broth to hot rice results in a hard, uncooked kernel in the center of the grain.)

Heat a second sauce pan to medium, put in oil & butter, pour in rice and coat it by stirring gently; let sit 2-3 minutes. Using a soup ladle, add one ladle of hot stock at a time, waiting for that liquid to be absorbed. Stir then add another ladle and continue until all stock is absorbed. Make sure the color of the rice remains pearly white by stirring often with a wooden spoon. Ensure that you do not burn the rice and that the liquid is being absorbed.

Cook vegetables as the rice is cooking. Heat a skillet to medium-high add oil and butter and sauté vegetables until onion becomes transparent. Add curry, honey, herb mixture and sauté for 2-3 minutes. Add pumpkin puree and 1 cup of stock stirring to combine with vegetable mixture. If mixture is too thick, add a bit more stock.

Once the risotto seems done, the rice should be mostly tender, but with just a hint of firmness. At that point add one more ladle of stock; this will result in a creamy texture and keep it from getting too dry. Add the cheese at the very end. Combine the rice and vegetable mixture and serve immediately.

Jeff serves this as a base and tops it with his Jumbo Shrimp with Walnut Pesto & Green Tabasco.

Note: the quantity of liquid suggested in this recipe is approximate; you may need a little more or less. Have extra hot water ready if you run out of stock.

RUBBED STRIPLOIN WITH CHILI PUMPKIN TOSTADA & WHITE AND BLACK SALSA

Go ahead and rub it in because when you do it enhances the flavour and adds real depth to this uncommonly good and very unique striploin dish.

serves 4

4-6oz. striploins
1 tbsp. canola oil

8-6" corn tortillas (store bought - also known as tostadas CHARRAS brand is good)
2 cups Monterey jack cheese, shredded

rub ingredients

2 tsp. sea salt
1 1/2 tsp. chili powder
1 1/2 tsp. onion powder
3/4 tsp. garlic powder
1/2 tsp. paprika
1/2 tsp. marjoram
1/4 tsp. ground cumin
1/4 tsp. ground black pepper
1/8 tsp. cinnamon

Mix rub ingredients in a bowl.

chili pumpkin mixture

4 tbsp. black olives, chopped
1 hot chili pepper,
    seeded and chopped
1 tbsp. olive oil
1 cup fresh pumpkin,
    cut into 1/2" cubes
1 tsp. paprika
1/4 tsp. cinnamon
2 tbsp. cilantro, chopped
sea salt and freshly cracked
    black pepper to taste

Prepare chili pumpkin mixture by heating a skillet to medium-high; add oil, pumpkin, chili, olives and chopped cilantro, sauté 2 minutes. Add paprika, cinnamon, salt and pepper. Remove from heat and set aside.

white and black salsa

1 cup black beans,
    cooked & drained
1 cup Great Northern beans,
    cooked & drained
1 cup tomatoes, diced
3 tbsp. white wine vinegar
1/4 cup cilantro, roughly chopped
1/4 cup red onion, chopped
2 tbsp. jalapeño pepper,
    seeded & chopped
2 cloves garlic, minced
1 tbsp. sugar
sea salt and freshly cracked
    black pepper to taste

Combine all ingredients in a bowl, stirring to mix. Set aside. Salsa recipe may make more than needed for this dish. Save and use for nacho chips!

method

Pre-heat oven to 400°F. Place striploin pieces in a bowl and coat with the rub. Heat skillet to medium-high; add 1 tbsp. canola oil and pan sear striploin on both sides to brown only. Place skillet in oven and cook to desired doneness.

Prepare white and black salsa; set aside. Prepare chili pumpkin mixture.

Lay a corn tortilla on each plate. Spoon 4 tbsp. of chili pumpkin mixture on the first tortilla and sprinkle with Monterey jack cheese and repeat for a second layer and heat in oven until cheese melts. Spoon the white and black salsa over the assembled tortilla. Lay cooked striploin alongside tortilla or on top to stack.

SALMON WRAPPED IN LIME COCONUT PANCAKES WITH RED CURRY SAUCE

Who needs rice with your salmon when you can have Lime Coconut Pancakes? Each salmon bundle is wrapped in a delicious coconut milk and zippy lime pancake. Add a dash of Red Curry Sauce and you have a mild yet complex flavour combination that begs to be savoured.

serves 4
4-4 oz. salmon fillets
1 tbsp. olive oil
1 tsp. dried red chili peppers
1 cup flour
1/4 tsp. salt
1 egg, lightly beaten
grated zest and juice of 1 lime
1 cup light coconut milk
sea salt and freshly cracked black pepper to taste

red curry sauce
2 tsp. red curry paste*
1 cup coconut milk
1/4 cup vegetable stock
1 tbsp. lime juice
1 tbsp. brown sugar
1/3 cup cilantro, chopped

Put all ingredients in a skillet on medium-high heat. Cook 4-5 minutes. Lower heat to simmer and cook for 10-15 minutes to reduce the sauce.

method
Make red curry sauce; set aside.

In a bowl sift the flour with a 1/4 tsp. salt. Make a well in the center and stir in egg, zest, lime juice and coconut milk. Whisk to a smooth batter. Season a large non-stick skillet and heat on medium-low. Spoon in batter to form a 6" diameter pancake. It may be helpful to shake or swirl pancake to spread it out. Cook about 2 minutes then flip to other side and cook 1-2 minutes more or until golden. Transfer to a platter and repeat until all pancakes are cooked.

Preheat oven to 325°F. Heat a skillet to medium-high, add oil, and salmon, flesh side down, and sprinkle with chilies. Sear salmon on both sides, remove from skillet and set aside. Place a salmon fillet on a pancake, roll up and put in the oven for 5 minutes. Serve immediately with the red curry sauce.

*If you cannot locate red curry paste, mix together: 2 tsp. yellow curry, 2 tsp. paprika and cayenne and dried red chilies to taste. Add enough vegetable stock to make a 'paste'.

GRILLED TILAPIA WITH TWO SALSAS

Not one, but two salsas help to enhance the flavour of delicate tilapia without overpowering it.

serves 4
4-6 oz. fillets of tilapia
2 tbsp. oil
1 tsp. of herb mixture (2 parts basil, 1 part oregano)
2 limes, cut in half
2 lemons, cut in half

tomato salsa
2 tomatoes, diced
10 basil leaves, chopped
2 tbsp. red onion, diced
1/2 tsp garlic, minced
3 tbsp. olive oil
1 tbsp. balsamic vinegar
1/2 tsp. coarse sea salt to taste

Mix all together in a bowl, set aside.

avocado salsa
1 avocado, diced
pinch of dried red chilies
1 tbsp. red onion, diced
3 tbsp. fresh lime or lemon juice
1/2 tsp. course sea salt
1/4 cup cilantro leaves
1 tbsp. olive oil

Mix all together in a bowl, set aside.

method
Make salsas.

Prepare tilapia by rubbing fillets with oil, basil and oregano. Grill approximately 2 minutes per side. Grill lemon and lime for garnish.

Plate tilapia and add salsas to the top. Garnish with lemon and lime.

Be careful grilling, these are usually small thin fillets and you don't want to handle them on the grill too much. Add salt and pepper to taste. Note: A "grill basket" helps to hold fillets together. They are available in many stores.

SEASIDE ORZO PASTA WITH LOUISIANA OYSTERS, TEXAS WHITE SHRIMP & MUSSELS

This dish has a decidedly coastal feel thanks to a bounty of oysters, shrimp, and mussels. Orzo, the versatile rice-shaped pasta, is a brilliant match for this seafood recipe especially when it gets an extra kick from pungent saffron, lemon zest, and parmesan cheese. The great thing is that you don't have to live by the ocean to enjoy it. Most grocery stores have a selection of fresh seafood all year round.

serves 4

2 cups orzo pasta, par-cooked
2 tbsp. olive oil
12 saffron threads
1 cup vegetable stock (store bought)
1/2 tsp. red chili peppers
3 fresh basil leaves, chopped
2 cloves garlic, minced
14 oz. canned & chopped tomatoes, with the juice
8 shrimp, peeled, deveined and tail removed
12 mussels, cleaned
8 oysters, shucked with juices
1/2 white onion, cut in half, put cut side down and cut into slices
1 can baby corn
2 tbsp. lemon zest
1 handful parsley, chopped
freshly grated parmesan cheese
sea salt and freshly cracked black pepper to taste

method

Soak* or infuse the saffron threads in the 1 cup of vegetable stock, set aside. Heat a heavy skillet to medium-high, add oil, onion, garlic, red chili peppers; sauté a minute or so. Add saffron infused vegetable stock, par-cooked pasta, chopped basil leaves, chopped tomatoes & juice, corn pieces, lemon zest, and parsley. Cover and cook for 2 minutes; add the oysters, shrimp and mussels and continue to cook until all the mussels have opened. (Discard any mussels that do not open.) Serve with cracked pepper and freshly grated parmesan cheese.

*Soaking the saffron in the vegetable stock is an important step to release aroma, flavour and colour to the dish.

Shucking oysters: Drape a towel over your open palm and hold the oyster. Using a shucking knife is most helpful, they are available in most grocery stores or seafood markets. Hold the knife in the hand without the towel. Slip the knife blade between the top and bottom shell right by the hinge on back. Carefully run the knife around the oyster until you get to the other side. Twist the knife and pry the oyster apart, saving the liquid inside. Sever the oyster free from the shell.

SPICY ONTARIO LAMB MEATBALLS WITH FRESH GARLIC, CUCUMBER YOGURT & CHIPOTLE SAUCE

Ontario lamb is the focus of this delectable dish. While garlic, cucumber yogurt, and chipotle sauce won't overpower the delicate lamb they do add a welcome hit of flavour.

serves 4

1 lb. ground lamb
   If you do not see ground lamb in the meat counter, ask the butcher to grind up lamb that has 20% fat content
1 onion, diced
1 1/2 tbsp. olive oil
2 garlic cloves, smashed
1 1/2 cup whole wheat breadcrumbs
1 egg
1/4 cup fresh parsley, chopped
sea salt and fresh cracked black pepper to taste
1/2 tsp. dried basil
1/4 tsp. dried oregano
1 tsp. cumin
4 oz. feta cheese, crumbled
3 oz. chipotle sauce (tabasco makes a good chipotle pepper sauce)

method

Preheat oven to 400°F. Place the following ingredients in a large mixing bowl; garlic, ground lamb, onion, cumin, egg, parsley, spices, whole wheat breadcrumbs, 2 oz. chipotle sauce and the crumbled feta cheese. Mix together with a spoon or your hands. Fill another bowl with warm water, set aside. Form meatballs by first dipping your hands into the warm water then picking up meat mixture to form even sized balls of desired size*. Heat a large ovenproof skillet to high; add oil and meatballs, arranging the meatballs in single layer in the pan. Quickly sear meatballs over high heat, and then place in the pre-heated oven, cooking until the meatballs are well browned and firm to the touch, approximately 8 to 10 minutes.

*Cocktail size meatball is: 3/4 – 1 oz. and dinner size meatball is: 1 1/2 – 2 oz.

cucumber yogurt

1/4 of a cucumber, sliced lengthwise into strips
1/2 cup plain yogurt
2 tbsp. fresh mint, chopped
juice of 1 lime
sea salt and freshly cracked black pepper to taste

Mix together in a bowl.

assemble

Place meatballs on a serving platter, dollop cucumber yogurt over meatballs followed by sprinkling chipotle sauce on top of the yogurt.

This dish pairs well with couscous and vegetables. It's hearty enough for winter dining but you may want to enjoy it anytime you see fresh lamb at the meat counter.

THAI SHRIMP CAKES WITH BANANA SALSA AND SPINACH WALNUT STIR-FRY

Try Thai cooking for the sense of accomplishment that comes from preparing an unfamiliar cuisine. Thai food is a great way to start being more adventurous in the kitchen and the real reward comes in eating it. Jeff used ingredients found in the local grocery store. You've got no excuse not to give it a 'Thai.'

serves 4

shrimp cakes
2 tbsp. canola oil
1 lb. raw shrimp, tail removed, peel, deveined and sliced lengthwise, chopped
1 tbsp. gingerroot, grated
1 green onion, chopped
1 tsp. fish sauce (store bought)
1/2 tsp. garlic chili pepper sauce (store bought)
1 cup watercress, chopped
3/4 cup Panko breadcrumbs
4 lime slices for garnish

banana salsa
1 large firm-ripe banana, peeled & sliced into 1" pieces
1 tsp. oriental sesame oil
1/2 cup golden raisins
2 tbsp. fresh cilantro, chopped fine
1 tsp. grated lemon peel
2 tsp. Thai roasted red chili paste (store bought)
1/4 cup sweet red peppers, thinly sliced
1/4 cup yellow peppers, thinly sliced

Mix all the ingredients for the banana salsa together and set aside for the flavours to blend.

spinach & walnut stir-fry
1 tbsp. walnut oil
1/2 cup California walnuts
1 small onion, cut in half, lay on cut side & thinly sliced
4 tbsp. pineapple, diced
4 cups fresh baby spinach
sea salt to taste

Heat a skillet to medium-high; add walnut oil and onions and sauté one minute. Add pineapple and walnuts sautéing another minute or two until the pineapple gets hot. Add the spinach and salt; sauté one minute.

method
Preheat oven to 400°F. In a mixing bowl put shrimp, ginger, onion, fish sauce, chili sauce, watercress, and 1/4 cup of the Panko breadcrumbs. Mix together. Shape into 2 oz. cakes. Coat both sides of each cake with crumbs. Heat ovenproof skillet to medium-high; add oil. Sear shrimp cakes to a golden brown on the first side, turn over and place the skillet in the hot oven. Finish shrimp cakes in the oven until they are cooked through, approximately 10 minutes.

To assemble, remove the shrimp cakes from oven and place on a platter, garnish with lime slices. Serve with the Banana Salsa and Spinach & Walnut Stir Fry.

WHOLE WHEAT SPAGHETTI WITH GARLIC CREAM SAUCE

Cream makes for a rich sauce that's a nice counterpoint to the simple taste of whole-wheat pasta. Go with the classic version or add some body to the dish with Jeff's favourite fresh veggie mix.

serves 4

2 cups cooked whole wheat spaghetti*
2-3 cloves garlic, minced
2 tbsp. olive oil (slightly more if incorporating vegetable option below)
2 tsp. herb mixture (2 parts basil, 1 part oregano)
1 cup whipping cream (35%)
1/2 cup vegetable stock (store bought)
2 cups Jeff's favourite vegetable mixture
8 tbsp. parmesan cheese, grated
8 chive stems, washed and patted dry
4 'flowers' of fresh cilantro
sea salt and freshly cracked black pepper to taste

method

In a large heavy pan, heat oil to medium, add garlic and Jeff's vegetable mixture and sauté. Add vegetable stock, herbs and cream, turn heat to high and bring to a boil. Add cooked spaghetti and allow the cream to reduce and thicken slightly as it continues to cook down. Season with salt and pepper to taste. Serve in warmed pasta bowls and garnish with chives and sprinkle with parmesan cheese.

*Cook spaghetti by bringing 4 to 5 quarts of salted water (1 tsp. of salt per gallon of water) to a rolling boil. Slowly add the pasta to the boiling water. Ideally, the water should not stop boiling. To keep pasta from sticking, stir during the first minute or two of cooking. Do not add oil. It keeps the sauce from sticking to the cooked pasta. Quickly drain the pasta and let it stand in the colander just long enough to drain.

ingredients for vegetable mixture (Use your favourite combination of vegetables)

- red onion, sliced thinly
- zucchini, cut into quarters lengthwise and diced
- green, red and yellow peppers, cored, cut into 1/4 inch strips and chopped
- mushrooms cut into quarters
- turnip, julienne 1/2 inch thick
- eggplant, cut into 1/2 inch slices and diced

ONTARIO LAMB WITH KIWI, PECAN & PEAR SALSA AND LENTIL POPPADUMS

There is a global feel to this stellar recipe. Jeff combines quality local lamb with kiwi, curry, and mellow mint yogurt. Layering the lamb with salsa and crisp poppadums is a treatment that makes this lamb dish something very special.

serves 4

1 lb. Ontario lamb sirloin (4 oz. per serving, 3 medallions per person)
juice of 2 limes (or lemons)
2 cloves garlic, minced
2 kiwi, peeled and crushed
1 tbsp. liquid honey
1 tsp. curry powder

Make marinade: Mix lime juice, kiwi, curry and garlic, set aside. Trim all fat from lamb. Cutting across the grain, cut lamb into 12 medallion slices. Flatten medallions with a mallet. Pour marinade over lamb and allow to marinate 2-6 hours.

pecan and pear salsa

1/2 cup pecans, roughly chopped
juice of 2 limes
1 pear, halved, cored and roughly chopped
1/2 cucumber, seeded, halved and then sliced
4 kiwis peeled and cut into 3 wedges
2 tbsp. fresh mint, chopped
1/2 red onion, finely diced
2 tbsp. fresh coriander, washed & chopped

Mix all ingredients in a bowl. Set aside.

yogurt sauce

2/3 cup plain yogurt
1/2 tsp. sea salt
1 tsp. fresh mint, chopped

Mix all ingredients in a bowl. Set aside.

poppadums

4 poppadums (store bought)
2 oz. oil

Heat skillet with oil. Place individual poppadum and fry for 30 seconds per side. Remove from pan and set aside.

method

In a large heavy skillet, heat 1-2 tbsp. oil, add the marinated lamb and sauté 3-5 minutes or until lamb is cooked to preferred doneness. (Jeff prefers medium-rare)

Let's put everything together...on the plate:
Layer poppadums with equal amounts of lamb and salsa. Drizzle with a little of the kiwi pan juices and top with the yogurt.

MEDITERRANEAN TOMATO AND WHITE BEAN STEW WITH ROASTED VEGETABLES, SWEET CHILI & CORN FRIED STUFFED JALAPEÑO

This fragrant Tuscany inspired stew is 'full of beans' and simmers with great flavour. It's comfort food all grown up.

serves 4

1-2 tbsp. olive oil
1 cup canned white beans, drained
4 cups of fresh vegetable mixture (see below)
2 tsp. herb mixture (2 parts basil, 1 part oregano)
2 cloves garlic, minced
1 large tomato, diced
1 48 oz. can crushed tomatoes
1 can of tomato paste
sea salt and freshly cracked black pepper to taste
1/4 bottle of chipotle sauce
1 tsp. red chili pepper flakes
1/4 cup demerera sugar
1 cup diced cooked potatoes, optional

method

Heat a heavy stockpot to medium-high.
Add oil, garlic, and vegetable mixture. Sauté until onion turns translucent. Add white beans, tomato, crushed tomatoes, tomato paste, chili pepper flakes, chipotle sauce, and demerera sugar. Add cooked potatoes at this point if desired. Bring to a boil; reduce the heat to low and simmer until the stew is heated through. Check seasonings and adjust if desired. Garnish each bowl of stew with corn fried stuffed jalapeños.

corn fried stuffed jalapeños

2 jalapeños, cut in half lengthwise
(remove seeds and membrane)
4 tbsp. ricotta cheese, strained of any liquid
1 tbsp. lime juice
Pinch of sea salt to taste
freshly cracked pepper to taste
1 egg, whisked lightly in a bowl (used as an egg wash)
1/2 cup corn flour (used to dredge peppers)
canola oil for frying

method

You should have 4 jalapeño halves. Mix together the ricotta, lime juice, salt and pepper. Divide the cheese filling into quarters and pack the filling tight against the jalapeño cavity. Dredge each of the four stuffed jalapeños in the corn flour. Dip each one in the egg mixture then back again into the corn flour. Set aside. Heat canola oil to medium-high in a small heavy skillet. Carefully place stuffed jalapeños into the hot oil and fry one minute on each side. Place each stuffed jalapeño half on top of a bowl of stew and serve.

ingredients for vegetable mixture (Use your favourite combination of vegetables)

* red onion, sliced thinly
* zucchini, cut into quarters lengthwise and diced
* green, red and yellow peppers, cored, cut into 1/4 inch strips and chopped
* mushrooms cut into quarters
* turnip, julienne 1/2 inch thick
* eggplant, cut into 1/2 inch slices and diced

SHRIMP CREOLE GUMBO

Without a doubt this is the most famous dish in the city of New Orleans. As common as red beans and rice on Monday, shrimp Creole can be found on any table in Louisiana for Friday lunch.

serves 6
2 pounds (21-25 count) shrimp, peeled and deveined
1/4 cup vegetable oil
2 cups chopped onions
2 cups chopped green peppers
1 cup chopped celery
Creole seasoning to taste (see below)
4 cups peeled, seeded and chopped canned tomatoes
1 tbsp. chopped garlic
2 tbsp. flour mixed with 1/4 cup cold water
1 cup vegetable stock (store bought)
2 bay leaves
1/2 cup sliced green onions,
sea salt and freshly cracked black pepper to taste
Louisiana hot sauce to taste (store bought)

method
In a 2-gallon heavy bottomed stockpot, heat oil over medium-high heat. Add onions and sauté 2-3 minutes. Add green peppers and celery, and sauté an additional 2 minutes or until vegetables start to wilt. Season to taste with Creole seasoning (see below). Stir in tomatoes and garlic, and sauté 2 minutes. Add flour mixture and stir. Simmer 2 minutes or until sauce starts to thicken. Pour in vegetable stock and bay leaves. Bring to a boil and reduce heat. Simmer 20 minutes. Add shrimp and cook 2-3 minutes. Add green onions, salt pepper and hot sauce. In New Orleans this dish is commonly served over rice.

creole seasoning
2 tbsp. onion powder
2 tbsp. garlic powder
2 tbsp. dried oregano leaves
2 tbsp. dried sweet basil
1 tbsp. dried thyme leaves
1 tbsp. black pepper
1 tbsp. white pepper
1 tbsp. cayenne pepper
1 tbsp. celery seed
5 tbsp. sweet paprika

Combine in a food processor and pulse until well blended, or mix thoroughly in a large bowl. This recipe doubles or triples well.

SPICY MACEDONIAN PORK & LEEK SAUSAGE PATTIES WITH SUNDRIED TOMATO AND SPINACH COULIS

Traditional Macedonian cuisine combines Balkan and Mediterranean traits, which were influenced by Turkish tastes that prevailed during the Ottoman rule. The Pork & Leek Sausages, Sundried Tomato and Spinach Coulis, exemplify the region and its traditions.

serves 6

24 oz. ground pork, 12 2 oz. patties
3 tbsp. extra virgin olive oil
1/2 cup leeks, washed and chopped fine using both the white and green part
1 tbsp. sea salt
1 tsp. red chili peppers
1 tsp. black pepper
2 tbsp. garlic, minced
1 tbsp. dried thyme
1/4 cup fresh parsley, chopped
1/4 cup cilantro
grainy mustard for garnish (store bought)

method

In a mixing bowl add all sausage ingredients except the grainy mustard and thoroughly mix together. Shape into patties about 2" in diameter and 1" high. It is important not to 'overwork' the meat as it being mixed together and shaped. Heat an oven-proof skillet to medium-high; place shaped patties in the hot skillet, brown first side, turn over and cook another minute them place the skillet in the oven to roast until meat is cooked, approximately 15 minutes. Resist the urge to press down the patties; this produces a less juicy product.

sundried tomato & spinach coulis

3 tbsp. extra virgin olive oil
1/4 cup red onion, finely chopped
1/2 cup red pepper, diced
1/4 cup zucchini, chopped
3 cloves garlic, minced
2 cups canned tomatoes, chopped
1 tsp. tomato paste
3 tbsp. sundried tomatoes in olive oil, chopped
   (store bought)
1/2 tsp. dried oregano
1 1/2 tsp. basil
sea salt and freshly cracked black pepper to taste
1 cup canned lima beans, rinsed and drained
1 1/2 cup of baby spinach, roughly chopped
1/4 cup flat-leaf parsley, chopped

method

Heat a heavy saucepan to medium-high; add oil, onion, red peppers, spices, garlic and zucchini; allow vegetables to sauté without flipping or stirring until onion on the bottom softens and becomes translucent. Add stock, tomatoes, tomato paste, sundried tomatoes and bring to a boil. Reduce heat and simmer uncovered 20 minutes, stirring occasionally. Add the spinach, beans and parsley and cook another 10 minutes.

Remove the patties from oven and plate. Serve with sundried tomato and spinach coulis and dollop with grainy mustard.

OVEN ROASTED CHICKEN BREAST SKIN STUFFED WITH RICOTTA, MARJORAM AND LEEKS SERVED WITH CRANBERRY RELISH & GRILLED APPLES

This roasted chicken is moist and brimming with flavour. Mellow ricotta, aromatic marjoram, and sweet caramelized leeks nestle under the crispy skin. The perfect accompaniment is Jeff's Grilled Apple and Cranberry Relish.

serves 4

4-6 oz. boneless chicken breasts with skin on, washed and patted dry
1/4 of a leek, chopped fine
2 cloves garlic, minced
1/2 tsp. dried oregano
1 tsp. dried basil
1/2 cup ricotta cheese
pinch of sea salt
4 sprigs of fresh marjoram (or 1 tsp. dried)
1/2 tbsp. + 2 tsp. of olive oil
1 green apple, cut into slices
whole berry cranberry sauce (store bought)

method

Preheat oven to 375°F. Heat a skillet to medium-high. Add 1/2 tbsp. of olive oil and chopped leeks and sauté until the leeks become translucent. Remove from heat and cool slightly. Mix together the leeks, garlic, oregano, basil, ricotta cheese and salt. Set aside.

Take the chicken breasts and lift the skin away from the meat of the cut side only. Stuff 2 tbsp. of cheese mixture under the skin of each breast spreading the mixture as evenly as possible. Lay a fresh sprig of marjoram over each breast (or a tsp. of dried marjoram). Drizzle each breast with 1 tsp. olive oil. Place chicken in an ovenproof dish and roast in the oven for 30 minutes or until chicken is cooked. Take apple slices and place in with chicken, when there is 5 minutes remaining of the roasting process.

Plate chicken with apples and serve 2 tbsp. of cranberry sauce with each breast.

CURRY STEW

You won't miss the meat one bit in this flavourful Middle-Eastern inspired dish.

serves 6

3 tbsp. garlic puree
2 pinches basil and 1 pinch oregano
2 oz. cooking oil
1/4 turnip cut into sticks
4 medium potatoes, par cooked and cubed
1 red onion, chopped
3 ounces mushrooms, quartered
1 each, green, red, and yellow pepper, chopped
2 zucchini, chopped
6 cups vegetable velouté
3 tsp. curry powder
1 tbsp. olive oil
1/2 cup raisins
1/2 cup diced fresh pineapple
1/4 cup sliced almonds, roasted
1/4 cup shredded sweet coconut
6 tbsp. chutney (store bought)
1/2 cup plain yogurt
6 tbsp. frozen blueberries

vegetable velouté

7 cups vegetable stock (good quality available in tetra packs in grocery stores, preferably without MSG)
1 cup all purpose flour

Pour cold stock into a large saucepan reserving a 1/2 cup of the stock, and bring to a boil. Using the 1/2 cup of the stock, whisk the flour into the cold stock until it is absolutely smooth. Take the flour mixture and pour slowly into the hot stock, stirring constantly. Reduce to simmer as velouté thickens in approximately 10 minutes.

blueberry yogurt

Mix yogurt and blueberries together in a bowl.

method

In a hot pan add oil, garlic, herbs, vegetables and pineapple; sauté. Add veloute and raisins and heat. Stir in curry powder and cook for 30 minutes on medium heat. Serve in individual bowls. Add 1 tbsp. of blueberry yogurt and 1 tbsp. of chutney per bowl. Sprinkle roasted coconut and almonds over each portion.

MUSHROOM RISOTTO WITH SHIITAKE AND BUTTON MUSHROOMS, SWEET ONIONS, GARLIC AND HERBS

Melt in your mouth mushroom risotto combines the intense flavour of shiitake with the earthy taste of button mushrooms. Add sweet onions, garlic, and herbs for a dish that's remarkably smooth and decidedly delicious.

serves 4

2 cups shiitake mushrooms, washed & stems removed
2 cups button mushrooms, washed & sliced
1 cup arborio rice
4 tbsp. olive oil
7 cups vegetable stock (good quality available in tetra packs at grocery stores, preferably without MSG)
1 large red onion, diced
4 cloves garlic, minced
1/2 tsp. dried oregano
1 tsp. dried basil
4 tbsp. butter
1/2 cup fresh grated parmesan cheese
1 cup fresh spinach, cut into ribbons

method

In a saucepan heat the vegetable stock. Keep it warm as you make the risotto.

Heat a large heavy skillet to medium-high. Add two tablespoons of oil and rice to the skillet. Stir rice for two minutes to 'coat' with oil. Add 1/2 cup of warm vegetable stock, stirring constantly until the liquid is absorbed into the rice. Repeat this process always adding 1/2 cup warm stock at a time until the rice becomes starchy and soft. Remove from heat and set aside.

In a separate skillet, heat to medium-high. Add the remaining two tablespoons oil, both kinds of mushrooms, herbs, garlic, and onion. Sauté until mushrooms are soft. Add the mushroom mixture into the cooked rice and stir. Add the butter and parmesan cheese and stir. Divide the mushroom risotto onto four plates and garnish each plate with fresh spinach ribbons. Serve immediately.

PO'BOY SANDWICHES

The famous Po'boy sandwich originated in New Orleans but it's a treat that anyone can enjoy anywhere in the world with a little instruction. Start with a fresh baguette with a thin tender crusty outside and moist airy inside. Jeff uses chicken but you can use oysters, shrimps, catfish, or any other type of meat. "Dress it" with sauce and enjoy!

makes 4 sandwiches

ingredients
1/2 cup hot sauce
8 slices red onion
8 slices tomato
1 cup lettuce, shredded
2 baguettes – whole wheat or white,
    cut in half and hollowed out (pull out excess bread)
2 cups slaw
4-4 oz. corn floured chicken

corn flour chicken
1/2 tsp. thyme
1 tsp. salt
1 1/2 cups corn flour
2 eggs, whipped
4-4 oz. chicken breasts, pounded to 1/2 inch thick,
    and cut in half lengthwise
2 oz. oil

method
In a bowl mix corn flour, thyme and salt. Whip eggs in a second bowl. Dredge each chicken breast in corn flour, dip in egg mixture, and dredge again in the corn flour. Ensure that the chicken is coated top and bottom. Preheat oven to 375°F. Add oil to frying pan and heat. Add chicken and brown each side. Place chicken in oven for approximately 10 minutes to complete the cooking process.

hot sauce
1/4 cup ketchup
2 tbsp. worcestershire sauce
1/2 tbsp. dry hot mustard
1 tbsp. Cajun spice
2 tbsp. water
1 tbsp. herb mix

method
Mix all ingredients in a bowl, stir and refrigerate.

slaw
2 cups cabbage, shredded
1/4 cup hot sauce
1/2 cup mayonnaise

method
In a bowl stir mayonnaise and hot sauce together. Add cabbage and mix.

assembly
Put lettuce in hollowed out bread. Add 2 tbsp. of hot sauce per sandwich. Add the onions and tomatoes. Add 4 tbsp. of coleslaw per sandwich. Place the corn flour chicken into the sandwich and cut sandwich in half to serve.

CATFISH SEARED WITH TANDOORI AND CUCUMBER LIME YOGURT

Catfish is reported to be the most widely eaten fish in America. You won't be surprised, once you've tasted it. The white meat is firm yet delicate with a mild but distinctive flavour. Spice things up with a hit of tandoori seasoning and then mellow the flavour with cooling cucumber yogurt.

serves 4

4-8 oz. catfish fillets, washed and patted dry
1/4 cup tandoori seasoning* (sometimes referred to in grocery stores as tandoori barbeque)
3 limes cut in 1/2
1 tsp. dried basil
1/2 tsp. dried oregano
4 tbsp. canola oil for frying
12 x 2 inch long by 1/8 wide strips of cucumber for garnish

cucumber lime yogurt

1/2 cup plain yogurt
1 lime, juiced
1/4 seedless cucumber, chopped
sea salt and freshly cracked black pepper to taste

Put cucumber and lime juice in the bowl of a food processor. Start to whirl and add in yogurt. Do not over process. Set aside.

tandoori spice seasoning

4 tsp. curry
1 tsp. ginger
1/4 tsp. cinnamon
2 tsp. paprika
1/4 tsp. garlic powder
1/2 tsp. cumin
1/2 tsp. salt

Mix all together. Set aside.

method

In a bowl combine tandoori spice and herbs. Dredge each fillet on both sides in the tandoori spice. Heat a large heavy skillet to medium-high. Add oil. Place catfish in skillet, flesh side down. Fry two minutes; gently flip fillets over to the second side and fry two more minutes. Remove pan from heat.

To serve, place two tablespoons of the cucumber lime yogurt on top of each fillet. Lay a lime slice against the fillet and three strips of cucumber on top of the cucumber lime yogurt.

desserts

ALMOND PLUM TARTS

Little Jack Horner would love these plum tarts! The taste is pure and simple and the pastry-free tarts are ready to eat in just minutes.

serves 4
4 oz. butter
1/2 cup icing sugar
2 eggs
1 tsp. vanilla
3/4 cup almonds, sliced
1/3 cup all purpose flour
4 plums, washed and pits left in

method

Preheat oven to 350°F. Brush a little canola oil in 4 ramekin dishes and place a plum in each ramekin. Cut a 'star' (cut an x + a horizontal line) in each plum.

In a bowl, beat together butter, icing sugar, flour and eggs and beat until blended; add vanilla. Pour mixture over the plums and bake for 25 minutes or until the plums are softened and tart is cooked.

Spread slivered almonds in an ovenproof skillet in a single layer. Bake them in a preheated oven for 12-15 minutes, or until light or golden brown and set aside.

Remove plum tarts from the ramekins, cut in half and garnish with sliced almonds.

APPLE & RAISIN DATE CAKE
WITH CINNAMON YOGURT CREAM

This moist cake has a taste of mysterious Morocco thanks to the dates, yogurt and exotic spices that infuse it with flavour.

serves 6

1/2 cup dates, chopped
2 1/2 cups tart apples, sliced
1/2 tsp. salt
1/4 tsp. nutmeg
1 1/2 tsp. cinnamon
1 tsp. baking soda
1/2 cup low-fat buttermilk
1 cup unsweetened applesauce
1/4 cup honey
1/4 cup demerera sugar
3/4 cup granulated sugar
1/2 cup light corn syrup
1 egg white

cinnamon yogurt cream sauce

1 cup vanilla yogurt, low fat
2 tsp. cinnamon

Put all above ingredients in a bowl and stir.

method

Preheat oven to 350°F. Combine honey and demerera sugar in a non-stick skillet. Cook over medium heat until the sugar dissolves, 2-3 minutes. Add the apples, dates and continue to cook, stirring often until the apples begin to soften, (about 3-4 minutes.) Remove from heat. Lightly spray the sides and bottom of a 9 inch springform pan. Put the fruit mixture into the pan. In a large bowl, put in sugar and corn syrup, beat with electric mixer at medium speed until blended. Add egg white and beat on high until mixture is smooth. Add applesauce and buttermilk and continue beating on high for 1 minute. Combine remaining ingredients and add them to the batter. Mix until smooth. Spread the batter evenly over the fruit.

Place the pan on a baking sheet and bake on the middle rack of the oven for 40-45 minutes. (a toothpick inserted into the center of the cake should come out clean) Remove cake from oven and cool on a rack, approximately 15 minutes. Use a butter knife to run around edges of pan. Invert the cake onto a serving platter. Pour cinnamon yogurt cream sauce over cooled cake.

FROZEN CHOCOLATE MARSHMALLOW PIE

Calling all chocoholics! It's always the right time to indulge when you love chocolate. This chocolate lover's dream is a heavenly way to end any meal.

serves 12

454 grams mini marshmallows
200 grams of semi-sweet chocolate squares (reserve 1 block for shaving as garnish)
1/2 cup store bought chocolate fudge sauce (use a good quality)
1/4 cup 35% whipping cream (to be added to marshmallows)

3/4 of a 350 gram bag of Oreo cookies

3 cups 35% whipping cream
1 tbsp. icing sugar

method

Fill bottom of double boiler with water and place on low heat. In a bowl, place (all but one) of the chocolate squares, marshmallows, fudge sauce and 1/4 cup of whipping cream and place on top of the double boiler. Allow ingredients to melt, stirring occasionally. Do not cover. Remove mixture from heat and quickly cool the mixture by placing the bowl of marshmallows into another bowl of ice (see below).

While mixture is cooling, put the Oreo cookies in a food processor and whirl until crumbly. Press cookie crumbs into a 9" pie pan; set aside. Whip the 3 cups of 35% cream & icing sugar together. Fold the whipped cream into the cooled marshmallow/chocolate mixture. Pour mixture into crust. Chill 2-4 hours in the freezer.

When ready to serve, grate the one reserved square of chocolate into shavings. Cut and serve each piece of pie and sprinkle with chocolate shavings.

hints on whipping cream

*Begin with thoroughly chilled cream
*Chill mixing bowl and beaters
*Use metal bowl or glass to whip cream

using an ice bath

An ice bath can be very effective for cooling heated foods. Fill a large bowl with ice and a small amount of water. Place the hot chocolate/marshmallow dish in the bowl of ice. Stir mixture frequently to avoid hot spots and to enhance cooling. Be careful not to 'slop' any of the ice water into the chocolate mixture.

BANANA SOUR CREAM CHEESECAKE WITH WALNUT GRAHAM CRUST

You'll swing from the trees when you taste Jeff's walnut graham crusted banana cheesecake. Cream cheese and yogurt are infused with banana and poured into a crunchy walnut graham crust. The flavour and texture are a perfect complement to one another. Go bananas!

serves 8

walnut graham crust

1 1/2 cups graham cracker crumbs
1/2 cup ground walnuts (pulse in the food processor a few times)
3 tbsp. sugar
6 tbsp. unsalted butter, melted

method

Preheat oven to 325°F. Combine the graham cracker crumbs, walnuts, and sugar in a food processor and whirl to combine. Add the butter and stir until all the ingredients are moistened. Spread the mixture into an ungreased 9" pie plate (or 9-inch spring form pan). Use your hands or a flat-bottomed glass to press the mixture evenly into the bottom and sides (if desired) of the pan. Bake 8 to 10 minutes, until golden brown and firm. Remove from the oven and set aside to cool.

banana sour cream cheesecake

1 lb. cream cheese
1/2 cup granulated sugar
1 lemon, squeezed of juice
1 cup bananas, mashed (approximately 3 bananas)
2 eggs
1/2 cup plain yogurt

method

Increase oven temperature to 350°F. In a large mixing bowl, beat the cream cheese, sugar and lemon juice together. Add the eggs, one at a time, beating well after each addition. Stir in the yogurt and mashed bananas and blend well until smooth. Pour the mixture into the prepared crust and bake for 1 hour. Turn off the oven. Cool in the oven, with the door propped open until cake is at room temperature. Serve.

CANTALOUPE MERINGUE PIE

Melons are abundant at the Crescent City's Farmer's Market in N'awlins. In this recipe Jeff uses cantaloupe to make a wonderfully refreshing pie. It's a perfect way to finish a meal but if you can't wait until dinner, enjoy a slice with your afternoon coffee.

serves 8

1-9" deep-dish pastry shell, baked
2 cups cantaloupe, peeled
3/4 cup evaporated milk
1/8 tsp. sea salt
1/4 cup butter
2 tsp. pure vanilla extract
1 cup sugar
1/4 cup cornstarch
1/4 cup cold water

method

Preheat oven to 350°F. Puree cantaloupe in a food processor. In a saucepan combine 1 cup of sugar and cornstarch and heat. Gradually stir in cold water and evaporated milk until smooth. Stir in the beaten egg yolks and bring to a boil. Remove from heat. Stir in lemon peel and juice, vanilla, butter and cantaloupe. Let cool and pour into prepared shell. Add meringue (see below) and bake for 15 minutes or until the meringue is lightly browned.

meringue

3 egg whites
(separate whites & yolks in two separate bowls)
1/2 cup sugar
1/2 tsp. cream of tartar

In a metal bowl (never plastic) add egg whites, and whisk on a medium speed for several minutes until foamy. Continue whisking with the mixer and slowly add 1 cup of sugar and cream of tartar, beating on high until soft peaks hold their shape.

CARAMEL PECAN DUMPLINGS

Tantalize your taste buds with these tempting little treats that melt in your mouth. Using the self-rising flour makes them a breeze to make. The maple walnut frozen yogurt is perfect with these dumplings so make an effort to track it down at your local grocery store.

serves 6

ingredients for dumplings
1 1/4 cups self-rising flour
pinch of salt
2 tbsp. butter
1/2 cup sugar
1 tsp. pure vanilla extract
1/3 cup milk
1 cup pecan halves, roughly chopped

ingredients for sauce
2 tbsp. butter
1 cup demerera sugar
1 cup water

method
Sift the flour and a pinch of salt into a bowl. Using your fingertips, rub in the butter until the mixture is fine and crumbly. Add chopped pecans and mix together. Make a well in the centre of the combined mix. Then whisk egg, milk and vanilla in a separate bowl and pour the mix into the well. Stir to form a soft dough.

Make the caramel sauce by melting the butter in a skillet, adding the sugar and carefully pour in water. Stir over medium heat until combined and the sugar has dissolved. Bring the mixture to a boil, and then gently drop the dough by tablespoons into the sauce. Cover and reduce the heat to a simmer. Cook for 15-20 minutes, or until a knife inserted into a dumpling comes out clean. Spoon dumplings onto serving plates and drizzle with the caramel sauce.

Serve with frozen maple walnut yogurt (available in grocery stores).

CHOCOLATE CAKE WITH FUDGE SAUCE

If you like chocolate, you'll love this cake! It's moist, double chocolate-y and not too sweet. A store bought fudge sauce is okay in a pinch but Jeff's version is worth the little extra effort.

serves 10

1/2 cup cocoa
1 cup boiling water
1/2 cup butter
2 cups all-purpose flour
2 cups sugar
1 1/2 tsp. baking soda
1 tsp. salt
2 eggs
1/2 cup plain yogurt
1 tsp. vanilla
fudge sauce (use your favourite store bought version or prepare the recipe that follows)

method

Preheat oven to 350°F. Grease and flour a cake pan. Mix cocoa, boiling water and butter until dissolved. Allow mixture to cool. In a bowl, combine flour, sugar, baking soda, and salt. Slowly mix the dry ingredients into the cooled cocoa mixture. Add eggs, one at a time, beating well after each egg is added. Add the plain yogurt and vanilla. Pour batter into pan and bake 35-40 minutes or until a toothpick comes out clean. Remove from oven and cool.

Once cake has cooled, slice and put on individual serving plates. Pour some of the hot fudge sauce over each piece of cake. Serve.

fudge sauce

3 tbsp. unsalted butter
1/2 cup water
1/3 cup 35% cream
2 tbsp. liquid honey
1/2 lb. bittersweet chocolate, coarsely chopped (or use your favorite dark chocolate bar with 70% cocoa content)
1 1/2 tsp. vanilla

Melt the butter in a heavy saucepan. Add water, cream, and honey and bring to a simmer over moderately high heat. Put the chocolate pieces in a medium, heatproof bowl and pour the hot cream mixture over the chocolate. Wait approximately one minute, and then stir the mixture until smooth. Add vanilla and stir. Yields: about 1 1/2 cups.

BAKED BANANAS
WITH VANILLA BEAN AND YOGURT

This sweet treat is packed with grown-up taste but you may feel tempted to lick the plate like a kid when it's gone. Rumour has it this is not a dessert you'll want to share.

serves 4

4 bananas with skin on, washed and sliced lengthwise
1 vanilla bean
zest of 1 orange
2 tbsp. orange juice
4 tbsp. demerera sugar
3 tbsp. butter
1 cup vanilla yogurt (store bought)
2 tbsp. green pistachios, shelled, roasted and finely chopped
4 tsp. roasted coconut shavings
fresh mint to garnish

method

Heat a heavy skillet to medium-high; add butter and brown sugar and melt. (Stoves vary; so be careful not to burn the butter and sugar.) Place banana halves, vanilla bean and orange zest in skillet, sprinkle with pistachios, and sauté 2-3 minutes. Add orange juice to pan and sauté another minute or so.

Gently place warmed bananas on serving plate, drizzle with pan sauces, sprinkle with coconut shavings and dollop vanilla yogurt on top of bananas. Garnish with fresh mint.

DATE & PECAN PUDDING WITH HOT BUTTERSCOTCH SAUCE

The results are in and this dessert clearly wins the prize in the moist and delicious sweepstakes. Just one taste will have you going back for more.

serves 6
1 cup pitted dates, cut in half lengthwise and chopped
1 1/2 tsp. baking soda
5 oz. water, boiled
2 1/2 tbsp. unsalted butter
2/3 cup demerera sugar
2 eggs, beaten
1 tsp. pure vanilla
1 tbsp. candied ginger, chopped fine
1 cup self-rising flour
1/2 cup pecans, chopped

butterscotch sauce
1/2 cup cream
1/3 cup demerera sugar
2 tbsp. butter

method
Preheat oven to 350°F. Place dates in a deep bowl; sprinkle baking soda over dates. Pour boiling water over dates and let mixture stand until cool. (Mixture will foam.) Butter an 8" x 8" square baking dish. Whip sugar and butter until light and fluffy; add eggs, one at a time beating between. Add self-rising flour, pecans, ginger and vanilla and mix until ingredients are blended. Add the cooled date mixture and mix together until combined well. Pour batter into baking pan and bake 25-30 minutes or until done.

Prepare sauce while pudding is baking. Heat a heavy saucepan to medium-high. Add butter and sugar, mix together; add cream and cook until the sauce thickens. To serve, put pudding onto dessert plate and pour butterscotch sauce on top.

HAZELNUT MERINGUES
WITH SUGARED FIGS

Figs are lusciously sweet with a melange of textures from chewy flesh, to smooth skin, and crunchy fig seeds. Served with melt-in-the mouth meringues, this is a dessert that's both simple and sophisticated.

serves 6
6 fresh figs or dried, cut in quarters
4 tbsp. demerera sugar

12 tbsp. vanilla yogurt for extra sauce for figs

meringues
3 egg whites
1/2 cup (superfine) sugar
3/4 tbsp. cornstarch
3/4 tsp. white vinegar
1/2 oz. hazelnut extract

method
Preheat oven to 250°F. Line a baking tray with parchment paper. Place the egg whites in the bowl of an electric mixer and beat until soft peaks form. Gradually beat in the sugars, a little at a time and add hazelnut extract. Sift cornstarch over the mixture and fold thoroughly with the vinegar. Take 1 tbsp. of the mixture and shape into a small round on the baking tray. Repeat with the remaining mixture. Place the tray in the oven and bake for 30-35 minutes. Turn off the oven and allow the meringues to cool in the oven.

Press the cut side of the figs into the demerera sugar. Heat a non-stick frying pan over medium heat and add the figs. Cook for 2 minutes or until the sugar has melted and is golden.

Remove the meringues from oven and place on serving plates. Serve with a spoonful of yogurt and the figs on the side.

MAPLE CREAM TART
WITH ROASTED PECANS & WINTERMINT

Elegant and simple, the heavenly flavour of maple combined with the richness of cream and the just-right crispness of lightly roasted pecans makes this tart a wonderful ending to a perfect meal..

serves 6
1 /2 cup maple syrup
1 3/4 cups cream
2 tbsp. icing sugar
5 egg yolks
1 tbsp. cornstarch
1/2 cup pecans, roasted
8 sprigs mint

short crusted pastry
2 cups flour
5 oz. butter
2-3 tbsp. iced water
2 tbsp. sugar (dissolved in ice water)

method
Pastry: In a food processor blend the flour and butter until the mixture resembles fine breadcrumbs. While the motor is running, add enough sweetened cold water mixture to form a smooth ball of dough. Remove from processor. Knead dough lightly, put in plastic wrap and refrigerate for at least an hour, but preferably overnight. When ready to use, roll out pastry on a lightly floured surface to 1/4" thick and place into pie shell.

Preheat oven to 375°F. In a bowl, mix cornstarch and cream and all other tart ingredients thoroughly. Pour into pie shell and bake for 35 minutes or until set.

KIWI & CANTALOUPE FONDUE WITH HOT RASPBERRY SAUCE

Flashback to fondue. Enjoy the social experience as you dip your fondue fork loaded with fruit into warm raspberry sauce. This is a fun and tasty way for friends and family to make dessert time a 'groovy' experience.

serves 4
1 kiwi, peeled, cut into 3 slices
1 cantaloupe, cut into large chunks
12 fresh large blackberries

ingredients for hot raspberry sauce
1/2 cup icing sugar
1 tbsp. cornstarch
2 cups raspberries
1 lemon, squeezed for juice
1/3 cup cold water

method

Cook raspberries and sugar gently on medium heat until the berries lose their shape. In a bowl combine the cold water and cornstarch and whisk to blend. Add lemon juice to the hot berry mixture and stir. Pour in the cornstarch water and whisk until sauce cooks a few minutes and thickens. Pour in a fondue pot and keep warm.

Spear fruit with fondue fork and dip into the warm fruit sauce. (Almost any of your favourite fruits can be used with this fondue).

NECTARINE WALNUT FRITTERS WITH VANILLA YOGURT CUSTARD

Fritters have been common fare since the Middle Ages, but Jeff's fruit and nut concoctions have a decidedly modern twist. This hot, fresh fruit dessert is pure comfort food.

serves 4

3 medium nectarines, diced
1/2 cup pitted dates, coarsely chopped
1/2 cup California walnuts, coarsely chopped
1 1/4 cup whole wheat flour
3/4 cup brown sugar
1 tsp. salt
1/2 tsp. baking soda
1 tsp. baking powder
2 tsp. cinnamon
1 tsp. nutmeg
1 tsp. allspice
3/4 tsp. ground cloves
1 whole + 2 egg whites, beaten slightly
1/4 cup canola oil
2 tsp. sugar, optional

vanilla yogurt custard

1 cup vanilla yogurt
1 egg yolk, beaten
3 tbsp. honey

method

Vanilla yogurt custard: Heat the vanilla yogurt in a double boiler. Add the beaten eggs and honey and continue to stir occasionally until mixture thickens. Set aside.

Put nectarines, dates and walnuts in a large bowl. In a separate mixing bowl combine flour, brown sugar, salt, baking soda, baking powder, cinnamon, nutmeg, allspice and cloves. Stir in fruit and nut mixture tossing to coat evenly. Pour in beaten eggs and oil and stir until well blended.

Heat a large heavy skillet to medium, add oil for frying, Drop the batter by heaping tablespoons in to the oil, spreading it gently into an oval shape about 2 1/2 to 3 inches long. Avoid pressing or flattening the fritter with a fork. Cook for 2 1/2 to 3 minutes on the first side. Turn and cook for 2 minutes on the other side. The fritter is cooked when it has turned golden brown. You may need to add additional oil for each batch before frying. Serve on a platter with vanilla yogurt custard.

PECAN CHOCOLATE PIE
WITH CHOCOLATE CRUST & DRIZZLE

This deliciously decadent pie is filled to the brim with a sweet custard and pecan filling. The addition of rich chocolate makes every bite pure bliss.

serves 12

chocolate crust
1 cup all purpose flour
1/2 cup baking cocoa
6 tbsp. butter, chilled
1 tbsp. sugar
1/2 tsp. salt
2 tbsp. (or more) ice water

filling
4 oz. semisweet chocolate, chopped
2 tbsp. (1/4 stick) butter
1/2 cup (packed) demerera sugar
3 large eggs
1/4 tsp. salt
3/4 cup light corn syrup
2 cups pecan pieces, lightly toasted

method
Combine crust ingredients in processor. Using on/off turns, process until mixture resembles coarse crumbs. Process just until moist clumps form, adding more water by the teaspoon if mixture is dry. Scrape dough out of the bowl and form into a ball. Flatten into disk. Wrap dough in plastic wrap and refrigerate 30 minutes. (This step can be prepared 1 day ahead. Keep refrigerated.)

Preheat oven to 325°F. Roll out dough on floured surface to 13-inch round. Transfer to 9" diameter glass pie dish. Trim overhang to 1 inch; fold under and crimp. Set aside.

filling
Stir chocolate and butter in heavy small saucepan over low heat until melted. Remove from heat and cool slightly. In large bowl whisk brown sugar, eggs, salt and corn syrup and add to the chocolate mixture. Sprinkle pecans over the unbaked crust. Pour chocolate filling over pecans. Bake until crust is golden and filling is puffed (about 55 minutes). Cool pie completely on rack. Pour the chocolate drizzle in a zigzag pattern over the whole pie or over each individual serving (see below).

chocolate drizzle
6-1 oz. squares of semi-sweet chocolate
2 tbsp. butter

Put chocolate and butter in small heavy saucepan over low heat until melted. Use to drizzle over pie.

PEACH & BLUEBERRY SHORTCAKE

This dessert combines nearly caramelized fruit and melt-in-your-mouth shortcake. The dollop of vanilla yogurt takes it beyond the realm of ordinary shortcake.

serves 6

1/2 cup flour
3 tbsp. cornstarch
3 tbsp. brown sugar
1/2 tsp. ground ginger
1/2 tsp. baking powder
1 1/2 tbsp. unsalted butter, softened
1 egg yolk
1 cup blueberries
2 peaches, peeled & sliced
2 tbsp. superfine sugar
1/2 cup vanilla yogurt

method

Preheat oven to 325°F. Sift flour, sugar, ginger, salt and baking powder into a bowl. In a separate bowl whisk together butter and egg, add to dry ingredients and mix together making dough. The dough may become very stiff and slightly difficult to work. If the dough does not hold together, add a little cold milk or water until it does. Roll pastry out on a lightly floured surface. Cut into approximately 3/4-inch rounds with your favourite pastry cutter and place on an ungreased cookie sheet. Bake for 10-12 minutes or until pastry is lightly golden, being careful not to overbake. Remove from oven.

Heat a heavy saucepan to medium-high; add blueberries, sugar and stir as mixture thickens and is almost caramelized. Add sliced peaches and heat until peaches begin to soften. Remove from heat; add vanilla and stir.

To assemble, lay a shortcake on the plate, spoon out some hot blueberry and peach mixture on top. Place a second shortcake on top of berries at a slight angle. Drizzle vanilla yogurt over shortcake, dust with icing sugar and garnish with a sprig of fresh mint.

FRESH RASPBERRY & BLUEBERRY WITH HOT LIME CUSTARD CREAM

Stirred custards are popular 'across the pond' and with good reason. They are easy to make and a deliciously light dessert. Jeff uses fresh raspberries and blackberries, for a flavour pop and a burst of colour. Like Oliver Twist, you'll be asking, "Please, sir, can I have some more?"

serves 4
1/2 cup milk
1 cup 35% crème
1 vanilla bean, split
5 egg yolks
7 tbsp. sugar
2 limes, squeezed for juice
fresh raspberries and blueberries to fill 4 stemmed glasses (or bowls) two thirds.

method

Put milk and cream into a sauce pan. Split the vanilla bean in half and scrape the seeds and vanilla pod into the milk/cream. Heat the mixture on medium heat until small bubbles begin to appear. Remove from heat. In a medium sized mixing bowl, beat together the egg yolks, sugar and lime juice until light and creamy. Remove vanilla pod from milk. Gradually pour the egg and sugar mixture into the milk and cream stirring continuously. Place the pan back on the stove on low heat and cook custard about 10-15 minutes, stirring constantly until the custard thickens yet remains a pourable inconsistency. When it's cooked, remove custard immediately from the heat to stop cooking. Place fruit in stemmed glassware (or bowls). Pour hot custard over fruit.

VANILLA BEAN PEARS WITH BLUEBERRIES & ROASTED WALNUTS

Don't look for leftovers here...there won't be any! The vanilla scented fruit and brown sugared walnuts are just too good to resist!

serves 4

4 firm, ripe pears, sliced
2 tbsp. fresh lemon juice
1 tbsp. butter
1 1/4 cups blueberries
4 tbsp. brown sugar
2 oz. walnuts
2 vanilla beans

method

Heat a heavy skillet on medium. Melt butter and add walnuts. Lightly brown walnuts, then add sugar and mix well to coat. Continue to cook for 3 minutes on medium heat. Add blueberries, pears, squeezed lemon juice and vanilla bean. Cook until juice is reduced and fruit begins to caramelize. Serve warm.

RASPBERRY AND PISTACHIO RICE PUDDING

Here's a twist on a retro dessert...and it's nothing like Grandma used to make. Jeff's rice pudding is rich and creamy, sweet and tart with a bit of pistachio crunch. Don't take our word; try it yourself. As they say, "the proof is in the pudding."

serves 4
1 tbsp. canola oil
2 cups whole milk
1 cup icing sugar
2 tsp. orange zest
1cup arborio rice
1/2 cup whipping cream (35%)
1 tsp. rosewater*
1/2 cup shelled pistachio nuts, roasted**
1 1/4 cups raspberries, washed and drained

method

Place oil in a heavy saucepan Add rice and stir well on medium heat. Add 1/4 cup milk and as it absorbs continue to add another 1/4 cup until all milk is used. Stir constantly. When all the milk is in, add sugar and orange zest. Remove from the heat and cool slightly. While rice is cooling, whip the cream. Fold whipped cream and rosewater into the rice when the rice has cooled. Spoon a layer of rice pudding into the serving dish, sprinkle on some raspberries, spoon on another layer of rice and finish with more raspberries and pistachios.

Why use arborio rice? It has a smooth and creamy consistency that makes the rice pudding silky and rich.

*Rosewater is available in bulk and health food stores. It sweetens the rice pudding with a refreshing natural flavour.

**To roast pistachios, put shelled pistachios on a baking pan and in bake at 325°F, stirring occasionally until they're slightly golden, about ten minutes.

TOFFEE APPLES
WITH CINNAMON RAISIN YOGURT

This dessert rocks! A sweet toffee shell encases a tender poached apple, which is topped with creamy cinnamon raisin yogurt. Make this dessert before you go to work or even the night before but add the yogurt cream just before serving. Serve at room temperature, if it's been made ahead of time.

serves 6
6 small apples, peeled
1 cup white sugar
4 cups water

toffee
1 1/2 cups demerera sugar
1/2 cup water

yogurt topping
1 tsp. cinnamon
1/4 cup raisins
1 cup yogurt

method
Mix yogurt, cinnamon and raisins together, set aside.

Place apples, water and white sugar in a saucepan over medium heat, and poach for 4 minutes or until the apples begin to soften, but still have some crunch. Remove from water and put on a rack to cool and dry.

To make toffee, heat saucepan on low heat, add demerera sugar and water and stir until sugar dissolves and turns a golden colour. Pour toffee over the apples and place on parchment paper for 5 minutes to set.

Serve with the yogurt topping.

VANILLA BEAN CUSTARD
WITH GRILLED RUBY RED GRAPEFRUIT

Savour the sensation of biting into chilled vanilla bean custard that's been topped with warm ruby red grapefruit. Cool your palate with the gentle hint of fresh mint.

serves 4

4 tbsp. icing sugar
1 cup cream
1/2 cup milk
1 vanilla bean
1/2 tbsp. gelatin
1 1/2 tbsp. water
2 ruby red grapefruit, peeled & divided into slices
zest of an orange
1/2 tbsp. butter
fresh mint to garnish

method

Pour cream, milk and vanilla bean into a saucepan and heat on a medium setting. Stir and add orange zest and 2 tbsp. of the icing sugar for the grapefruit and continue to heat. Put water in a separate bowl and sprinkle unflavored gelatin over the water; stir gently but thoroughly with a spoon until the gelatin is completely dissolved. Pour into the saucepan with the cream mixture and heat until mixture thickens, stirring occasionally. Pour custard into individual cups and chill.

Heat a small skillet on medium-high; add butter, prepared grapefruit slices and the remaining 2 tbsp. of icing sugar and sauté quickly until they are lightly browned. Spoon the warmed grapefruit over the custard and garnish with fresh mint.

YOGURT FRUIT CRÈME BRULE

Jeff's take on the classic crème brule takes four fruits, yogurt, and brandy to come up with a new and delicious twist on an old favourite.

serves 4

1/2 cup strawberries
1/2 cup raspberries
1/2 cup blackberries
1/2 cup vanilla yogurt (store bought)
1 oz. metaxa*
2 tbsp. demerera** sugar
2 sprigs fresh mint

method

Pre-heat oven to broil. Wash, drain and dry off all the berries. Divide fruit evenly into four ovenproof shallow bowls. Spoon the yogurt over the top of the fruit. Sprinkle demerera sugar over the yogurt. Drizzle metaxa over the fruit mixture. Place bowls on a shallow baking dish and put in oven under the broiler until the sugar caramelizes. Remove baking pan with bowls from oven. Bowls are hot; take precautions in handling. Garnish each serving with a fresh sprig of mint. Serve.

*Metaxa is a blend of brandy, three wines and rose petals. It is a distilled and aged product with a sweet & mellow taste.

**Demerera sugar is a natural, unrefined brown sugar with the rich aroma of tropical sugarcane. It offers rich taste with caramel flavour notes and has a crunchy texture.

BANANA CREAM PIE
WITH COCONUT CRUST

It's hard to decide what to eat first, when the piecrust is as delectable as the banana crème filling. Together they make a first-class dessert.

serves 8

crust
2 cups flaked coconut
1/4 cup butter

Melt butter in a large skillet over medium low heat; add coconut and sauté until golden brown. Press mixture into the bottom and up the sides of greased 10-inch pie pan. Bake at 350°F for 7 minutes. Remove from oven.

filling
3 tbsp. cornstarch
1/4 tsp. salt
3 cups half and half cream
4 egg yolks, lightly beaten
3/4 cup sugar
1/4 cup flour
1 vanilla bean
2 tbsp. butter, cut into small pieces
4 large firm ripe bananas, sliced and tossed with 11/2 tbsp. lemon juice
2 cups 35% whipping cream

In a heavy saucepan whisk cornstarch, salt and half and half cream. Place on stovetop and bring mixture to the boiling point. Set aside. Place egg yolks in mixing bowl and beat on medium speed of electric mixer, gradually adding sugar. Beat for 2 minutes, until mixture is thick and lemon-colored. Beat in flour on low speed, gradually add the cream mixture. Transfer mixture to heavy saucepan; add vanilla bean and heat over medium heat, stirring constantly. Let mixture come to a boil for about 1 minute, stirring constantly.

Remove from heat and continue to beat until mixture is smooth. Beat in butter a little at a time. Allow mixture to cool. In a separate bowl beat 1cup of the cream until firm but not stiff. Mix about 1/2 cup of the whipped cream into the cream mixture to lighten it. Add sliced bananas and transfer filling to the pastry shell. Refrigerate until serving time.

To serve; cut into slices and dollop with the reserved whipping cream.

UPSIDE-DOWN APRICOT SYRUP CAKES

Topsy-turvy, upsy-daisy or upside-down; call it what you will but these six little cakes with piping hot caramelized fruit on the bottom, a super moist centre and a topping of hot syrup are delicious. This is an upside-down cake that's decidedly upscale.

serves 6

caramelized fruit
1 cup brown sugar
1/8 cup water
2 tbsp. butter
1 cup dried apricots, chopped

4 dried apricots, cut into ribbons for garnish

cake batter
2 eggs, room temperature
1/2 cup sugar
1 tsp. vanilla
1 cup all purpose flour
1 tsp. baking powder
1/4 cup butter, melted
1/3 cup milk
1/4 cup of sliced hazelnuts

Place the eggs, sugar and vanilla in the bowl of an electric mixer and beat for 8-10 minutes or until thick and pale. In a bowl mix the flour and baking powder together. Add flour mixture to the egg mixture. Fold in melted butter, milk and hazelnuts. Set aside.

method
Preheat oven to 350°F. Grease a 6 muffin pan.

Place the butter and brown sugar in a saucepan over low heat and stir until the sugar is dissolved. Increase the heat and boil until syrup is a golden brown colour and slightly caramelized, about 5-8 minutes. Add chopped apricots and water and continue to cook until the apricots have soaked up the water and the topping has taken on the consistency of a caramelized sauce.

Pour equal amounts of the caramelized fruit into each greased muffin cup. Spoon the batter over the hot topping. Bake 20-25 minutes or until done. Remove from oven, cool for 2 minutes then invert the muffin pan onto a wire rack to finish cooling the little cakes. Garnish the top of each cake with 4 sliced apricot 'ribbons'.

24 CARAT CARROT CAKE

Sweet pleasure is delivered in every bite of this ultra moist, exceedingly delicious carrot cake.

serves 12

cake ingredients

1 cup California walnuts toasted and coarsely chopped
2 1/2 cups raw carrots, finely grated
1 cup all purpose flour
1 cup whole wheat flour
2 tsp. baking soda
1/2 tsp. baking powder
1/2 tsp. salt
1 1/2 tsp. ground cinnamon
5 large eggs
1 cup demerera sugar, packed
3/4 cup canola oil
2 tsp. pure vanilla extract
3 tbsp. applesauce
1 cup crushed pineapple, drained
2 cups golden raisins

cream cheese frosting

1/4 cup butter, room temperature
8 oz. cream cheese, room temperature
2 cups icing sugar
1-2 tsp. pure vanilla extract
zest of one lemon
1/4 cup vanilla yogurt

garnish options

1 cup unsweetened flaked coconut, toasted
    or 1/2 cup California walnuts, toasted and chopped

cake method

Preheat oven to 350°F. Place rack in center of oven. Butter or spray two 9" round cake pans and line the bottoms of the pans with a circle of parchment paper. Toast the California walnuts for about 8 minutes or until lightly browned and fragrant. Let cool and then chop coarsely. Peel and finely grate the carrots. Set aside. In a separate bowl whisk together the flour, baking soda, baking powder, salt, and ground cinnamon. Set aside. In bowl of electric mixer, using the paddle attachment, beat the eggs until frothy (about 1 minute). Gradually add the sugar and beat until the batter is thick and light colored (about 3-4 minutes). Add the oil in a steady stream and then beat in the vanilla extract. Add the flour mixture and beat just until incorporated. With a large rubber spatula fold in the grated carrots, applesauce, pineapple, raisins and chopped nuts. Evenly divide the batter between the two prepared pans and bake 25 to 35 minutes or until a toothpick inserted in the center comes out clean. Remove from oven and let cool on a wire rack. After about 5-10 minutes invert the cakes onto the wire rack, remove the pans and parchment paper, and then cool completely before frosting. Prepare frosting while cakes are cooling.

frosting method

In the mixer bowl using the paddle attachment, combine the cream cheese and butter on medium just until blended. Add the vanilla, lemon zest, vanilla, and yogurt and beat until combined. With the speed on low, add the powdered sugar in 4 batches and beat until smooth between each addition. Place the frosting in the refrigerator for 5 to 10 minutes before using.

To assemble: place one cake, top side down, onto cake platter. Spread with about a third of the frosting. Gently place the other cake, top of cake facing up, onto the frosting, and spread the rest of the frosting over the top of the cake. If desired, garnish with toasted nuts or toasted coconut.

YOGURT CRÈME, APPLE, PEAR & RAISIN PIE

Your friends will think you are sly to make such a great tasting pie!

serves 8

crust
1/2 cup whole wheat flour
1 cup rolled oats
1/2 tsp. cinnamon
1/4 cup apple juice
1/4 cup brown sugar

filling
5 cups sliced peeled apples (5-6 apples)
2 cups sliced peeled pears
1/4 cup brown sugar
1 cup low-fat yogurt
1/4 cup raisins
2 tbsp. whole wheat flour
1 tsp. cinnamon
1 egg, lightly beaten
1 tsp. vanilla

method
Preheat oven to 350°F. Spray springform pan lightly with vegetable oil. In a bowl combine 1/4 cup brown sugar, whole wheat flour, rolled oats, cinnamon, and apple juice. Pat one half of mixture into the bottom and sides of springform pan. Refrigerate.

In a bowl combine apples, pears, the remaining 1/4 cup brown sugar, yogurt, raisins, flour, cinnamon, egg and vanilla, toss together until well mixed. Pour into crust. Top with remaining crumb mixture. Bake 30-40 minutes or until topping is browned and apples and pears are tender.

BANANA SPLIT DESSERT

You've never tasted a banana split quite like this. It's the grown-up version of a summertime favourite that can be enjoyed all year round. It's easy to make and yet impressive enough to serve when company arrives unexpectedly.

serves 12

crust
2 cups graham cracker crumbs
6 tbsp. butter
Mix together and divide into 12 martini glasses or other fun glassware (Use a 9" x13" inch greased pan if you prefer)

filling
2 cups icing sugar
1/4 lb. butter (1/2 cup)
2 large eggs
3 bananas
19 oz. can (540 ml) crushed pineapple, drained
2 cups 35% very cold whipping cream + 2 tbsp. icing sugar
4 tbsp. sliced almonds (1 tsp. per serving) toasted (see below)
1 banana for garnish

method
In a bowl put icing sugar, 1/4 lb butter and eggs. Beat at high speed for 10 minutes. Spread the whipped mixture into each martini glass. Slice the 3 bananas over the top of the filling. Add a layer of crushed pineapple. Whip the cold cream vigorously adding the 2 tbsp. icing sugar towards the end.

Cream is whipped when it is billowy with soft droopy peaks. Dollop cream on the top of each 'Split' and garnish with 1 tsp. toasted almonds and banana slices. Another garnish option: Hot Raspberry Sauce (See Kiwi & Cantaloupe Fondue with Hot Raspberry Sauce recipe.) Serve chilled.

tips
* To achieve maximum volume when beating eggs, have them at room temperature.
* To toast almonds, place almonds in a single layer in a dry skillet, and turn heat to medium.
  Toast, stirring occasionally, until almonds are fragrant (2-5 minutes depending on the form of almonds you are toasting) but not burned.

PROFITEROLES

These French pastry bubbles are light and luscious. When they're stuffed with ice cream, sprinkled with coconut and raisins and drizzled with hot caramel pecan sauce they become irresistible.

serves 6
1 cup butter
1 cup water
4 large eggs
2 cups all purpose flour
caramel sauce (store bought or make your own)
1/4 cup coconut, lightly toasted
1/4 cup golden raisin
1/2 cup pecan halves, lightly roasted* and cut into pieces
18 small scoops of ice cream

caramel sauce
2 cups sugar
1/4 cup water
1/2 cup heavy cream
1 tsp. vanilla

Combine the sugar and water in a large heavy saucepan over medium heat. Cook, stirring with a wooden spoon until the mixture is a deep caramel color and looks like syrup, about 8 minutes. Carefully pour in the cream (it will bubble up) and continue to cook for another minute. Remove from heat and add vanilla. Allow sauce to cool slightly before serving.

method
Preheat oven to 275°F. Prepare cookie sheets by spraying with cooking spray or using parchment paper. In a medium saucepan bring butter and water to a simmer over medium heat. Add the flour and mix it to a dough-like consistency. It will come away from the sides of the saucepan as it turns to dough. Remove from heat and place dough in a food processor. Crack eggs into a small bowl. Begin to whirl the dough in the processor and add eggs one at a time until all 4 are fully blended. Drop a tablespoon of dough onto the prepared cookie sheet leaving enough room between them to expand. Bake at 275°F for 1 1/2 hours or until the profiterole buns are crisp, light and a rich golden colour. Pierce the side of each one to release steam and cool on a wire rack. While profiteroles are cooling, heat your favourite caramel sauce. (As an elegant option, add 2 oz. dark rum to the caramel sauce.) With a pointed and sharp knife, split the profiterole buns in half (horizontally). Place three profiteroles on each serving plate. Working quickly, place a small ball of ice cream in each profiterole and cover with the pastry lid. Ladle some warm caramel sauce over the profiteroles and sprinkle with the toasted coconut, pecans, and raisins. Serve immediately.

tips
• Roasting pecans: Preheat oven to 300°F degrees. Place nuts on a baking sheet in a single layer. Roast for approximately 7 minutes.
• Pecan Caramel Frozen Yogurt is excellent as the filling.
• Toasting coconut: Preheat oven 350°F. Place the shredded coconut on a baking sheet and place in oven. Stir every 30 seconds until the coconut is dry and mostly toasted light brown with some white shreds, about 2 to 4 minutes.
• Profiteroles can be baked and cooled 1 day ahead, then kept in an airtight container at room temperature.
• Bake in a preheated oven at 350°F for 5 minutes to restore crispness, before cutting and filling.

BANANA BREAD PUDDING
WITH VANILLA CINNAMON CREAM
& CARAMELIZED WALNUT SAUCE

Bread pudding is the ultimate in comfort food. Jeff's version has a gourmet twist that makes it destined to become a tradition in your family.

serves 8

12 cups stale French bread, cut into 1 inch cubes
5 eggs, separated (save the whites)
2 egg whites
5 1/2 cups whole milk
1 3/4 cups sugar
1 tbsp. vanilla extract
1 tsp. almond extract
1/4 cup dark rum
1/4 cup crème de banana liqueur
4 bananas, mashed
1 cup raisins
1 1/2 teaspoons cinnamon
2 tbsp. butter

walnut caramel sauce

4 tbsp. unsalted butter
1 cup dark brown sugar, packed
1 cup chopped California walnuts

vanilla cinnamon yogurt crème

1 1/2 cups vanilla yogurt
1 tsp. cinnamon

method

In a large bowl beat egg yolks with sugar until light yellow. Add milk, liquors, extracts, cinnamon and the mashed bananas, mixing well. In a mixer, beat the seven egg whites until stiff peaks form, then fold into the egg yolk mixture. Add the raisins, folding them in gently and being careful not to deflate the egg whites. Preheat oven to 350°F. Place the stale bread pieces into a large bowl, then pour half of the egg mixture over and mix well. Let soak for at least 10 minutes, then add the other half, and soak another 10 minutes.

Melt 1 tbsp. of butter and use it to coat a 9 x 9 x 3 inch baking dish. Pour the bread mixture into the dish, then cover with foil and place into a bain marie (or water bath — put the dish into a roasting pan and pour hot water into the roasting pan until it's about 2/3 the way up the side of the baking dish). Bake for one hour. Remove foil; finish baking until the center is set, about 15 more minutes (longer if necessary). Glaze the top of the pudding with 1 tbsp. of butter while it's still hot.

walnut caramel sauce

In a heavy skillet melt the butter, add the brown sugar and walnuts and cook over medium heat for 4 to 5 minutes until the sugar has melted and dissolved. Stir constantly and toss a few pinches of cinnamon; cook another minute.

Assemble: Slice the pudding into individual servings. Spoon some vanilla cinnamon yogurt crème onto a dessert plate and place a slice of banana bread pudding in the middle. Drizzle each serving with the walnut caramel sauce.

index

WHO'S COMING FOR DINNER • MORE FROM JEFF'S KITCHEN

index

index